A Ten-Lesson Bible Study

The God *of* All Comfort

Finding Your Way into His Arms
Through Scripture & Song

DEE BRESTIN

Companion Music CD Featuring Amy Shreve

ZONDERVAN®

ZONDERVAN.com/
AUTHORTRACKER
follow your favorite authors

ZONDERVAN

The God of All Comfort Bible Study Guide
Copyright © 2010 by Dee Brestin

Requests for information should be addressed to:

Zondervan, *Grand Rapids, Michigan* 49530

ISBN 978-0-310-94882-7

Cover design: Gayle Raymer
Cover photography: Gentl and Hyers / Jupiter Images
Interior design: Beth Shagene

Printed in the United States of America

09 10 11 12 13 14 15 • 24 23 22 21 20 19 18 17 16 15 14 13 12 11 10 9 8 7 6 5 4 3 2 1

To Steve

Contents

Sometimes a light surprises
The Christian while he sings;
It is the Lord who rises
With healing in his wings.
When comforts are declining,
He grants the soul again;
A season of clear shining
To cheer if after rain.

WILLIAM COWPER (1731–1800)*

*Kevin Twit has set Cowper's words to music on the CD
"Pilgrim Days: Indelible Grace II" (www.indeliblegrace.com).

Before You Begin

Instructions for Everyone

This Bible study differs from most Bible studies in that it is a study of Scripture *and* song. A musical CD featuring ten hymns performed by soloist and harpist Amy Shreve is included in the sleeve in the back of the guide. These hymns are integrally related to the passages you will be studying.

You do not have to read the book *The God of All Comfort* to do this study, but we certainly encourage it. In *The God of All Comfort* you learn, through Dee's moving story, how to cross "the bridge of lament" into the arms of God. In this Bible study, you will explore the hymns you can sing as you are crossing that bridge. These are two separate studies, and you can do both of them, or just one of them, but they do complement each other beautifully.

Instructions for Individuals

You do not need to be in a group to do this study. Each lesson is divided into five days. Each day, listen to or sing along with the hymn on the companion CD first, and then do the study, skipping the group icebreaker in the beginning and the group prayer time at the end.

Instructions for Groups

Do the five days as homework each week before you come to the study, listening to or singing along with the hymn each day. Your group facilitator will determine if you have time to answer all the questions in the discussion time, but you should prepare them all. Coming to the group with an empty guide is like showing up at a potluck empty-handed. Occasionally, that is understandable—but not as a regular practice. Star a few questions you might like to answer. For questions marked by an asterisk (★), Study Notes in the back of the guide are available if you are stumped—but don't look there too quickly! If you are naturally quiet, ask the Lord for courage to speak up. If you are naturally talkative, limit how many questions you will answer so that shyer members will have pauses in which to gather courage to speak up. Keep confidences in the group, and pray for one another during the week.

Instructions for the Group Facilitator

There are Leader's Tips for you in the back of this guide beginning on page 193.

It Is Well with My Soul*

When peace like a river attendeth my way,
When sorrows like sea billows roll;
Whatever my lot Thou has taught me to say,
It is well, it is well with my soul.

Though Satan should buffet, though trials should come,
Let this blessed assurance control;
That Christ hath regarded my helpless estate
And has shed His own blood for my soul.

It is well with my soul, it is well, it is well with my soul.

My sin, oh, the bliss of this glorious thought!
My sin, not in part but the whole,
Is nailed to the cross and I bear it no more,
Praise the Lord, praise the Lord, oh my soul!

It is well with my soul, it is well, it is well with my soul.

And Lord haste the day when the faith shall be sight,
The clouds be rolled back as a scroll;
The trump shall resound, and the Lord shall descend,
Even so, it is well with my soul.

It is well with my soul, it is well, it is well with my soul.

Words by: Horatio Spafford, 1873
Music by: Philip P. Bliss, 1876
Arr. by: Amy S. Wixtrom and Gary Wixtrom, 2008
©2009 G. B. WIX Publishing ASCAP

* Available on the companion music CD

THE CORDS OF DEATH ENTANGLED ME

(Hymn: "It Is Well with My Soul")

THOUGH JESUS TOLD US THAT IN THIS WORLD WE WILL HAVE TROUBLE, AND PETER TOLD US NOT to be surprised by suffering, still, when it comes, it feels like someone has punched us in the stomach. When I read over my prayer journal during our family's time of great suffering, I see gasping, stumbling, and cries of *Help! Help! Help!* The psalmist often uses the image of drowning to express his fears: the cords of death are entangling his legs and waves are breaking over his head. That's exactly how I felt the day we received our catastrophic news.

I was about to speak at a large retreat, after which two of my daughters and I would join my husband, Steve, and another daughter at the lake for an end-of-summer family vacation. Before his vacation, Steve decided to get a checkup—and to our enormous surprise, it revealed advanced colon cancer. The following are excerpts from that weekend's prayer journal.

Friday, August 1

Oh help us, Jesus. The sky has fallen. Steve called. It's not an ulcer. He has colon cancer. Please, please, please help us. I can't even imagine life without my gentle husband. No! O sweet Jesus, help us....

We're all crazy with fear. We're leaving now for the auditorium where I must speak. Be with us, O God.

Saturday, August 2

Somehow I got through the speaking. I'm sure it was dreadful—I felt like I was under water, the words coming out of my mouth like slow bubbles.

Afterward, Debbie *[the Indiana retreat coordinator]* told the women about Steve's diagnosis. An audible gasp. A thousand women stunned. Many wept. That scared me. He's not dying—is he, God? No—he can't be. He's in his prime.

And yet I know, we are but a vapor. Anyone. Anytime.

Oh God, help.

Debbie called the girls up so the women could pray for us. Sally broke down, bargaining with the women: "PLEASE, PLEASE, PLEASE pray for my daddy. I need him so badly right now in my life....

I knew I needed to get the girls off the stage. I whispered to them and they turned toward the steps, moving slowly, like shattered glass. I nodded to Kim Hill, and she moved quickly up, eager to rescue us, ready to lead the women in worship.

But oh—and I know You know—our hearts were so leaden it felt impossible to enter into worship. Annie was silent. Sally and I were weeping even while singing "It Is Well with My Soul." I had a fleeting thought of trying to be a better witness, but then a truer thought that You hate pretense and deceit of any kind.

So, the truth is, Mighty God, I bow to Your sovereign will, for I know You are Wisdom itself—but I am also afraid of what Your will might be. This is surely our Gethsemane.

GET ACQUAINTED

If you are hesitant to speak in a group, when your turn comes, simply say your name and then say, "Pass."

1. What is your name, and what do you hope to gain from this group?

2. Have you ever gone through such a frightening time that you felt the panic of one drowning? Share briefly.

DAY 1: THOU HAST TAUGHT ME TO SAY

Before Beginning Your Private Study, Sing:

Sing with your heart and mind before you begin your study. The most oft-repeated command in Scripture is "Praise the Lord," or "Sing to the Lord." And the most oft-repeated negative command in Scripture is "Fear not," or "Do not be afraid." There is a connection, and if you begin to obey the first, you will discover the power of singing praise in overcoming fear. You will also find your heart is more receptive to the Word when you study, for praise is like a spring rain that softens the soil.

Today, sing all of the verses of "It Is Well with My Soul" either with the companion CD or on your own. A contemporary praise song with a similar theme to this great hymn is Matt Redman's "Blessed Be Your Name." You can find it on the Internet or on iTunes. Sing it as

was so frightened and frozen. Yet, over these last four years, God has calmed me and warmed me. He has helped me to know that not just Steve, but his widow and his children, are being delivered to something better.

The lie that Satan always tells us is that God is not really good, does not really love us. When His children believe this lie, they falter. We see this throughout Scripture: Eve in the garden, the Israelites wandering in the wilderness, and Peter after the crucifixion. This is the lie, as Martin Luther puts it in "A Mighty Fortress," "that threatens to undo us." But while Satan is buffeting us with this lie, we can stand firm if we remember the truth, the truth that Horatio Spafford expresses so beautifully through his great hymn.

Meditate again on:

> Though Satan should buffet, though trials should come,
> Let this blessed assurance control;
> That Christ hath regarded my helpless estate
> And has shed His own blood for my soul.

23. As you contemplate the above:

    a. How does the scriptural truth of this stanza contradict the lie that God is not good and that He does not really love us?

    b. How does the building melody of this stanza complement the thought?

Meditate again on:

> My sin, oh, the bliss of this glorious thought!
> My sin, not in part but the whole,
> Is nailed to the cross and I bear it no more,
> Praise the Lord, praise the Lord, O my soul!

24. A corollary lie is that because of our sins we have lost God's love. So often following a catastrophic loss, Satan comes and whispers that we deserve it. There were things we could have done differently. And though that may be true, our mistakes do not cause us

to lose God's love. Why, according to the scriptural truth expressed in the above verse, have we not lost God's love?

At my husband's funeral, one of the first hymns we sang was "It Is Well with My Soul." The congregation was seated, and I was in the front row. But though I had felt frozen during the first three verses, when we came to this final verse hope rose in my heart, and I stood. The congregation of nearly one thousand followed my lead and finished the hymn triumphantly:

> And Lord haste the day when the faith shall be sight,
> The clouds be rolled back as a scroll;
> The trump shall resound, and the Lord shall descend,
> Even so, it is well with my soul.

25. As you contemplate the above:

    a. This day is described in 1 Thessalonians 4:13–18. Read the passage and write down its promises.

    b. How does the music complement the thoughts in the above verse?

26. If you read chapter 1 of the book *The God of All Comfort*, what stood out to you?

27. What particularly stood out to you from this week's lesson? From "It Is Well with My Soul"?

GROUP PRAYER TIME

Distribute index cards and ask each person to write down one personal area of pain or need in his or her life. (Ask them not to request prayer for others, but for themselves.) Then have them pass the card to the person on his or her right. That person should take it home and pray all week for that brother or sister. If time permits, cluster in groups of three or four, have each person read from the index card he or she has taken, and then have one or two support that need with sentence prayers. For example:

Kelly: *Lord, You see Mary's anxious soul. She's been laid off, in need of a way to pay her bills, and feeling depressed. Please be with her.*

Joe: *Yes, Lord—and please reassure Mary of Your care. Please be her Provider.*

(Pause)

Mary: *Lord, Joe is concerned about his sister's visit this weekend, for they have had a rough relationship. Please give Joe great wisdom during the visit.*

Kelly: *Yes, Lord. I agree. I ask for grace and healing.*

(Pause)

Psalm 131*

My heart is not proud, O Lord my Lord.
My eyes are not haughty, O Lord my Lord.
I do not, I do not, concern myself
With great matters or things too wonderful for me.

But I have stilled and quieted my soul, my soul.
Yes, I have stilled and quieted my soul, my soul.

Like a weaned child with its mother,
Like a weaned child is my soul.
Like a weaned child with its mother is my soul within me, Lord
O Lord my Lord.

Words from: Psalm 131
Music by: Amy S. Wixtrom, 1994
©1994 G. B. WIX Publishing ASCAP

*Available on the companion music CD

I HAVE QUIETED MY SOUL

(Psalm/Song: "Psalm 131")

GOD DREW ME OUT OF THE DEEP WATERS, AND I KNOW HE CAN DO THE SAME FOR YOU. THE WAY He came to me and showed Himself to me is the way He has come and shown Himself to suffering saints throughout the ages: "from Basil to Bonhoeffer to Bono,"[1] and yes, to Brestin, a simple daughter of God.

God spoke to me through the book of Psalms. That may not seem like a new idea, but what was new to me was *how* God intended me to use the psalms. I discovered that if you use the psalms incorrectly, you'll sink. Use them as God intended, and the Psalter sail will take you through the stormiest sea.

ICEBREAKER

When was the last time you cried to God for help?

DAY 1: THE LAMENT

Before Beginning Your Private Study, Sing:

The lament helps us hang onto God and keep talking to Him when we do not sense His presence or understand what He is doing. This week, in addition to learning Amy Shreve's "Psalm 131" from the companion CD, learn one lament and sing it as well. You can perfect "It Is Well with My Soul" or do another lament, such as one of the following:

Contemporary Laments (find them on iTunes or Google them)

"Hold Me, Jesus" by Rich Mullens

"Peace on Earth" or "Love Rescue Me" by U2 (rock)

"How Long?" by Michael Card

African-American Laments (in most hymnals or on the Internet)

"There Is a Balm in Gilead"

"Swing Low, Sweet Chariot"

Hymn Laments

"Abide with Me" (the eighth track on the accompanying
  CD is a song that is primarily "Abide with Me")

"Precious Lord, Take My Hand"

"I Need Thee Every Hour"

Or, learn just the chorus of "I Need Thee Every Hour"—you can find the melody on the Internet at www.cyberhymnal.org.

> I need Thee, O I need Thee ...
> Every hour I need Thee,
> O bless me now, My Savior, I come to Thee.[2]

Study:

Philip Yancey said that he had been told to go to the psalms for comfort, but when he did, he would end up reading one of the "wintriest psalms" and end up feeling "frostily depressed."[3] How comforting, for example, is this?

> Your wrath has swept over me;
>   your terrors have destroyed me.
> All day long they surround me like a flood;
>   they have completely engulfed me.
> You have taken my companions and loved ones from me;
>   the darkness is my closest friend.
>
> PSALM 88:16–18

But then Yancey came to understand that the Psalter is not a book *about* God, but a journal written *to* God. We do not read it like the other books of the Bible. Instead, we use it to help us dialogue with God. When we read the psalms, it's as if we are reading someone's prayer journal "over his shoulder."

If our prayers are honest, at times we will cry, *God, what are You thinking? Where are You?* The psalmist did this repeatedly, lamenting: "Why are you so far from saving me, so far from the words of my groaning?"[4] The Psalter is "rife with the pathos of praise and ethos of agony."[5] As author William Brown says, "The book of psalms captures better than any other corpus of Scripture the 'bipolar' life of faith."[6] Life is hard, God is mysterious, and right now we see "through a glass darkly." The Psalms, perhaps more than any other book of the Bible, help us see all these truths lived out.

When you are hurting, it is hard to pray, and even harder to sing. Upbeat songs can feel as abrasive as sand thrown in your eyes. But God has given us a way to talk to Him and even to sing to Him in the midst of despair. Not only David, but also Asaph, the psalmist who was a lead singer, wrote many laments. Asaph used the phrase "songs in the night," the songs that brought him comfort when his soul "refused to be comforted."[7] Throughout Christendom these are the songs—new and old—that believers have sung during suffering.

On the night of the Last Supper—the night His soul was overwhelmed with sorrow—Jesus sang a hymn with His disciples on the way to the garden of Gethsemane. When Paul and Silas were imprisoned, their legs cramping as they were held mercilessly still in stocks, they sang. One of the reasons that the African-American culture has contributed so richly to our heritage of inspirational music is because so many of those songs sprang out of deep injustice and suffering. Slaves sang as they worked from dawn to dusk; they sang to give themselves hope, and they sang to hang onto God.

We join in the pain and the hope of other believers when we sing as so many before us have sung—hymns and spiritual songs to remind us that in the midst of our loss, God is still good.

1. What did you learn about psalms from the above introduction?

2. What is a lament, and what is its purpose?

3. Give some examples from history and Scripture of believers using the lament.

In most of the lament psalms, there is a cry of anguish, but somewhere in the midst of the psalm the psalmist takes a turn—from reflecting on the difficulty of his own circumstances to reflecting on the goodness and the character of God.

4. Read Psalm 13.

    a. What four questions does the psalmist ask God in verses 1–2?

    b. What requests does he make of God in verses 3–4, and why?

    c. How do you see a turn in the psalmist's perspective in the closing two verses?

    d. Why do you think this turn happened?

5. Explain how "It Is Well with My Soul" is a lament with resolve.

DAY 2: I Will Never Leave You or Forsake You

Before Beginning Your Private Study, Sing:

Sing a lament. Then listen to Amy Shreve's version of "Psalm 131" and sing it with her.

Study:

On what would have been our fortieth anniversary, I sobbed a good part of the day. I was packing up the house to move from a home of sweet memories that I did not want to leave. The littlest things, like finding Steve's white surgery coat with his initials, SGB, on the pocket could cause me to crumble.

When I went to bed that night, I was fretful. When you are suffering deeply, you think the regular frustrations of life might call a truce for a while, but, of course, they don't. The toilet still overflows, the bills still pour in, and people — yes, even Christians! — can be difficult. Though I tried to sleep, anxieties multiplied, leaping over my pillow like bleating sheep.

I turned over on my side, looking at the vacant place where Steve used to be. *Oh, my darling — how could this have happened to us?*

Steve and I used to call each other "codependent insomniacs." If one of us awoke in the night, he (or she) would whisper to the other: "Are you awake?" When it was me, I knew that even if Steve was asleep, he would rouse to keep me company. If I was worried about something, he would listen to me pour out my heart, stroking my back, empathizing with his deep masculine voice, his calming ways.

Sometimes he would help me laugh about a trouble. Other times, when he knew there was no humor in a situation, he'd simply pray over me and hold me. If sleep still eluded me, he'd start quoting our favorite nursery rhyme:

> Winkin', Blinkin', and Nod, one night sailed off in a wooden shoe;
> sailed off on a river of crystal light into a sea of dew . . .

Safe in Steve's arms, our bed became a wooden shoe sailing off into a sea of dew — and I was lulled to sleep.

But Steve was not there. His side of the bed was achingly empty.

All of us have times of feeling alone, misunderstood, or betrayed. So often David felt that way and cried out: "How long, O Lord, how long? . . . All night long I flood my bed with weeping and drench my couch with tears."[8]

My cry that sleepless night was not nearly as eloquent as David's. I simply sobbed: *Help me, help me, help me, God!* I knew I needed God to be my Comforter, my Counselor, and my Husband — but that understanding exploded into a question: "But how do I connect with Someone who is not flesh and blood?" When I couldn't immediately sense God's presence, I curled up in the middle of our king-sized bed and wept. Without even realizing it, I had prayed a prayer of lamentation.

And a memory from the past came to me. I was twenty-one, trying to calm our firstborn in the middle of the night. He would awaken, hungry and howling. Though I would run to him and lift him from his crib, unbuttoning my nightgown as we settled in the rocker, he was too fretful to latch onto my breast. He would root about, but if he didn't find me in two seconds, he would rear back, his face red and contorted, his fists flailing. If I stroked his cheek, like the nurse in the hospital had told me to do, trying to coax him to turn toward me, he would erupt in anger, bursting into a horrific wail, one that I knew carried through our thin apartment walls. A mother's breasts respond to her baby's cry and my milk let down, ready for my baby—but his fretful state kept him from connecting with me. I kept thinking, *I'm right here, I'm right here!* A very long ten minutes later, he'd finally find me and nurse greedily. His perspiring face would relax, his eyes closing at half-mast in contentment. I would think, *Oh my, Pumpkin—what was all that about? I was right here.*

Suddenly, I identified. I was that baby, concentrating more on my distress than on the One who was right there. I sensed the Lord saying: *Dee, I am right here. I am right here.*

I stopped my fretting and fussing and was still. The chorus from an old hymn came to me, one I'd been listening to in a contemporary version, and I began to sing it softly, over and over again. In essence, it is the repeated cry of the psalms of lamentation:

> I need Thee, O I need Thee ...
> Every hour I need Thee,
> O bless me now, My Savior, I come to Thee.[9]

Gradually, my soul began to calm, my body began to relax, and my eyes went to half-mast ...

6. Describe Dee's "lament," and then, how God spoke to her.

The value of the lament is that it keeps us talking to God, keeps us in connection with Him. The temptation when we are facing trouble or sorrow is to back away from God. It isn't that we don't believe He exists, but we begin to wonder if He really loves us.

7. Meditate on Genesis 3:1.

a. How is Satan described?

b. What question does he ask of Eve?

★c. Look carefully at Satan's question and the spirit of it. What was Satan trying to get Eve to believe about God's character?

8. In Deuteronomy 1, Moses gives a sermon to the Israelites, reviewing their history.

a. What promise had God given to the Israelites through Moses, according to verse 21?

b. What lie did the Israelites believe? (v. 27)

c. When the Israelites were afraid that their enemies were too strong for them, Moses reassured them of God's care. Find all the ways he reassured them in verses 29–31.

d. How did the Israelites respond? (v. 32)

Often the reason we believe God "hates us" and has forsaken us is because we suspect He should. We know our own hearts. We know we are sinful, rebellious, and selfish, and so we think, *It makes sense that He would hate me.* But the good news of the gospel is that God's love does not depend on our behavior but on His character. You cannot speak this truth to your soul too often—in fact, you need to do so continually, to stand against the evil one who wants you to despair of God's love and goodness.

9. Describe how the good news of the gospel is articulated in each of the following passages:

    a. Deuteronomy 4:31

    ★b. Psalm 18

    c. 1 Peter 2:24–25

The value of the lament is that it keeps us connected to God. When we are overcome with fears, with feelings that we have been forsaken by Him, it allows Him to dialogue with us. If we clam up and back up, then we have cut off our lifeline. He wants us to be honest with ourselves, and we might as well tell Him what we are thinking, for He knows anyway. Truly, He longs to rescue us. His rescue might look different than the rescue we had envisioned, but He will indeed come.

10. Meditate on the following pictures from Psalm 18.

    a. How does the psalmist describe his plight in verses 4–5? If you were to paint this, what would you paint?

    b. Describe the psalmist's lament and God's response in verse 6.

c. Meditate on the word pictures in verses 7–19. Choose two, describe them in detail, and what each tells you about God's love.

DAY 3: DIALOGUING WITH GOD

Before Beginning Your Private Study, Sing:

Listen to Amy Shreve's version of "Psalm 131" and sing it with her. Begin to memorize it.

Study:

God spoke to me in my sorrow first through the memory He brought to me of my trying to calm our infant son. The next morning, He spoke to me again. This time it was through the Psalms, for it is my habit to pray through a psalm a day. That next morning, the psalm I "happened" to be on was Psalm 131. When I read it I knew that God was "kissing me." ("A kiss from the King" according to rabbinic tradition, is a living word from God.) God's living Word was confirming to me exactly what I had experienced from His Spirit the night before.

> I have stilled and quieted my soul;
> like a weaned child with its mother,
> like a weaned child is my soul within me.
> PSALM 131:2

By now it was very clear that God was answering my lament, was entering into dialogue with me. So I began to slow down, as I've learned I must do, and look carefully at the passage that was jumping out at me.

Psalm 131 is in the midst of a section called "The Psalms of Ascent," fifteen psalms that were sung by the Israelites on their pilgrimage to the temple in Jerusalem, psalms to prepare their hearts for meeting with God. Before we look at Psalm 131, it is important to look at the psalm sung just before it, Psalm 130—for Psalm 130 contains the cry to God, and Psalm 131 is the resolution.

11. With what cry does Psalm 130 begin?

This image is similar to one we've seen before, where the psalmist is sinking in the miry depths, and crying "Save me, O God, for the waters have come up to my neck" (Psalm 69:1). Derek Kidner writes, concerning the victim's terror: "What is clear in all such passages is that self-help is not the answer to the depths of distress, however useful it may be in the shallows of self-pity."[10] The good thing about real trouble is that we cannot help ourselves, but must cry out to God.

★12. In Psalm 130:3 we see the psalmist defeating the lie that Satan uses against us when we are in pain. See if you can discern it, and then state the truth as it is articulated in verse 4.

13. What resolution does the psalmist make in verses 5–6?

Rebecca St. James sings this psalm in a song entitled "More Than Watchmen." Find it on iTunes.

14. What reasons does the psalmist give Israel to put their hope in the Lord? (vv. 7–8)

15. What reasons do you have to put your hope in the Lord—even when He seems distant?

DAY 4: My Heart Is Not Proud

Before Beginning Your Private Study, Sing:

Sing Amy Shreve's version of "Psalm 131." Can you sing it by heart?

Study:

During a call-in program on Moody Radio's Midday Connection, author, counselor, and personal friend Jan Silvious had a particularly challenging call. She'd been encouraging the listeners, no matter their circumstances, to express thankfulness to God. The phone lines began to light up. The first call was from an angry woman. She enunciated each word loudly to try to penetrate what she perceived as Jan's denseness: *"GOD COULD HAVE STOPPED MY SON FROM TAKING HIS LIFE. I HAVE NO WORDS FOR GOD."*

I thought, *How are you going to handle this, Jan?*

Calmly, Jan said, "Then just say: 'No words, God. No words."

I smiled. *Right on, Jan. Right on.* For Jan was encouraging this woman, despite her great pain, to keep talking, to not let go of her only lifeline.

Not letting go of God is an act of humble faith. Though we may not understand God's ways, we can still trust Him. Some people feel that if they cannot understand the reason for suffering then God must not have one. In arrogance, they assume they are smarter than the One who made the universe.

In the story of Job, Job continually asks to have a dialogue with God so that God might explain why He has allowed all this suffering in Job's life. Finally, at the close of the story, Job gets what he has been asking for, for God comes to him out of the whirlwind.

16. What questions does God ask Job in the following verses?

   a. Job 38:4

   b. Job 38:31–33?

   c. Job 38:35

17. How does Job respond in Job 42:3?

18. Compare this to Psalm 131:1. What similarity do you see?

19. What do these Scriptures teach about what God wants from us when we don't understand His ways?

There are many kinds of deaths. Sometimes we are overwhelmed with sorrow because of the death of a dream. We wanted something so much, and it seems God is not going to give it to us. We've reasoned with Him: *I'd be a good mother!* But there is no baby. *I'd use my talent to glorify You!* But the doors keep closing.

We can feel as fretful as a baby who is in the process of being weaned from the breast. In biblical days, women nursed much longer than most western women do today, so weaning the child from the breast he had known and loved for years was extremely traumatic for that child. I nursed our firstborn only until he got teeth, but after that he was very dependent on a pacifier. It was weaning from the pacifier that was the challenge.

J. R. was three years old and had the plug in his mouth constantly. Sometimes he tried to talk around it. It was only when he ate that he would pull it out, holding it firmly in one hand while he ate with the other. It was pathetic. I had let it go on far too long.

I tried reason, telling him, "Sweetheart, big boys don't use pacifiers."

Confused, he said: "I'm a big boy—and I use a pacifier."

I finally bribed him with a red fire engine, making a trade. But when he realized the trade was permanent, the hysteria began. He pleaded desperately for days, hanging on my leg, trying to return the fire engine. When he realized I *still* wasn't going to return the pacifier, he collapsed on the floor with heartbreaking, breathless sobs. Though tempted to give in, I didn't, and one day, to my amazement, J. R. was content. He didn't ask for it. Now he could speak clearly, eat without removing the plug, and was being rescued, I hoped, from future braces.

When we don't get what we think we must have or when we lose what we think we have to have, we can become as frantic as the baby who loses the breast. We may think God doesn't know what He is doing. But in each case, He does. And in each case we need to be weaned. We need to realize that God longs to fill that void in our lives, and that He will do it even better than whatever He has allowed to be taken from us. The truth is, if we are that desperate about something else, even a good thing, it is probably a false god in our lives, squeezing out any room for the presence of the true God.

20. **VITAL QUESTION:** Go around the room, giving each person an opportunity to answer, "What, if taken from you or denied you, would make you feel desperate?"

21. What does this admission teach you about yourself? How is Psalm 131 relevant to you?

DAY 5: FOR I HAVE STILLED AND QUIETED MY SOUL

Before Beginning Your Private Study, Sing:

Sing Amy Shreve's version of "Psalm 131" by heart. Additionally, here are a few other suggestions to prepare your heart for today's lesson:

"The Solid Rock"
"You Are My All in All"
"It Is Well with My Soul"

Study:

Once the Lord reveals to us what we are clinging to instead of Him, we can begin the hard but valuable process of weaning. When our souls feel fretful, we must quiet them with the truth.

22. What does the psalmist tell Israel (or true believers) to do in Psalm 131:3?

23. Look back at your answer to question 20, for this will shine light into where you tend to place your hope other than Christ. Now, read Psalm 16 and use its truths to speak to your soul. As you meditate on these verses, write down a truth, and then pray God will help you release this false object of trust and to be content in His arms.

    a. What truth can you speak to your soul and pray from verses 1–2?

    b. What reassuring truth from God can you speak to your soul from verse 3?

    c. What warning can you speak to your soul from verse 4?

    d. What truth can you speak to your soul from verse 6?

    e. Ask the Lord to make the truths of verses 7–8 true in your life.

    f. What promises from verses 9–11 can you remind your soul of?

   Ask the Lord to remind you of these truths whenever you start to put your hope somewhere else.

24. If you read chapter 2 of the book *The God of All Comfort*, what stood out to you?

25. What do you think you will remember from this study? Why?

Group Prayer Time

Circle in groups of three and four for conversational prayer, using question 20 as your springboard. Each person should lift up the person or thing they tend to put their hope in rather than God. Then the others will pray for him or her, using truths from Scripture or songs based on Scripture. For example:

Mary: *Lord, I know that for me it is often what others think of me—I want the approval of others: my family, my friends.*

Ellen: *I'm like this too, Lord. But may Your pleasure become all that is really important to us, Lord.*

Joe: *Please be Mary's All in All. May that be true of each of us.*

Pause

Joe: *For me it's being able to take care of my family. Having a good job and staying healthy and alive so I can be there for . . .*

COME THOU FOUNT*

Come Thou Fount of every blessing,
Tune my heart to sing Thy grace;
Streams of mercy, never ceasing,
Call for songs of loudest praise.
Teach me some melodious sonnet,
Sung by flaming tongues above.
Praise the mount! I'm fixed upon it,
Mount of Thy redeeming love.

Here I raise my Ebenezer;
Hither by Thy help I'm come;
And I hope, by Thy good pleasure,
Safely to arrive at home.
Jesus sought me when a stranger,
Wandering from the fold of God;
He, to rescue me from danger,
Interposed His precious blood.

O to grace how great a debtor
Daily I'm constrained to be!
Let that grace now like a fetter
Bind my wandering heart to Thee.
Prone to wander, Lord, I feel it,
Prone to leave the God I love;
Here's my heart, Lord take and seal it,
Seal it for Thy courts above.

WORDS BY: ROBERT ROBINSON, 1758
MUSIC BY: JOHN WYETH, 1813
ARR. BY: AMY S. WIXTROM AND GARY WIXTROM, 1991 AND 2009
©2009 G. B. WIX PUBLISHING ASCAP

* Available on the companion music CD

46

SONGS
IN THE NIGHT

(Hymn: "Come Thou Fount")

THE PSALMS AND THE GREAT MUSIC OF THE CHURCH HAVE THE POWER TO DRIVE AWAY EVIL SPIRITS —those tormenting spirits that are trying to slip under every door and window. When we pray the psalms, when we sing the hymns, we slam the door or window on the slimy fingers of the enemy, causing him to slink back to the pit where he belongs.

In the Old Testament, both Job and Asaph (a psalmist and lead singer) talked about God giving "songs in the night." But we must ask Him for them—for these melodies that have the power to calm our heaving souls in the long hard nights that come to our lives. The first time I had the privilege to minister with Amy Shreve, the artist on your music CD, the conference began when the curtain opened to reveal a lovely young woman at a harp, who stroked the strings with long slender arms and plaintively pled:

> Come Thou Fount of every blessing,
> Tune my heart to sing Thy grace . . .

It was perfect. We cannot, in our own strength, tune our hearts. We can only plead to the Song-giver. That opening helped us turn from ourselves to the "Fount of every blessing." We were asking Him to come, to tune our hearts . . . and He did. He will do the same for you as you sing this prayer, this perfect petition, for it is in the center of His will.

This hymn is as rich theologically as a triple fudge cake. Too much too fast isn't wise or even possible, so most of the study will concentrate on the first verse. Later we will take a few more bites from the second and third verses. Give this lesson the time it merits, for it is foundational to this whole study.

Can you remember a time when music ministered to you? Did it play a part in bringing you to Christ, teaching, calming, or strengthening you? If possible, share one specific memory of a song that impacted you, and explain why it did.

DAY 1: COME THOU FOUNT OF EVERY BLESSING

Before Beginning Your Private Study, Sing:

Using the companion CD, sing with Amy in your own private place, listening and looking for the melancholy sounds, the plaintive pleas, and the sense of ongoing moral and emotional danger in "Come Thou Fount."

Study:

We are desperate for God, whether we realize it or not. This hymn writer is acutely aware of his desperation and his inability to help himself, so he continually cries out to the only One who can tune, rescue, bind, and seal a wandering heart. And he talks to his soul, reminding her (the soul is usually feminine in Scripture, perhaps to portray her vulnerability) of God's faithfulness in the past.

"Come Thou Fount" may not initially seem like a lament, but like "It Is Well with My Soul," it is a lament with resolve. It is filled with the long "ou" and "o" sounds that are common in a lament. Some renditions of "Come Thou Fount" are much more upbeat, but I feel they have missed the pleading lament in the hymn.

1. Overall observations:

    a. What pleas to God do you find in this song—either obvious or hidden?

b. What melancholy "ou" or "o" sounds stand out to you?

c. What evidence can you find for the songwriter's awareness of his continuing need?

d. How does he remind his soul of God's faithfulness in the past?

2. In the first verse, the writer seems to be calling on each member of the Trinity to help him. To whom do you think he might be referring and why when he mentions:

a. The "Fount" of every blessing (see John 4:13−14)

b. The "flaming tongues" above (see Acts 2:1−4)

c. The "mount" (see Psalm 87:1−3)

A mountain is representative of mystery, majesty, and foundation. Mount Sinai is where God the Father gave the Law; Mount Calvary is where He gave His only begotten Son to satisfy the requirements of the Law.

There is a key phrase in the first verse, a phrase we will explore carefully in the next few days. It is:

Teach me some melodious sonnet sung by flaming tongues above.

Psalms, hymns, and spiritual songs have power because they are:

- Melodious—the power of music
- Sonnets—the power of poetry
- Sung by flaming tongues above—the power of the Holy Spirit

3. If possible, share one thing you know or have experienced about the power of:

a. Music

b. Poetry

c. The Holy Spirit

DAY 2: THE POWER OF MUSIC ("TEACH ME SOME *MELODIOUS* . . .")

Before Beginning Your Private Study, Sing:

Prepare your heart today by singing "Come Thou Fount" along with Amy. Spend some time memorizing the first verse. Then, with a hymnal, or by finding it on the Internet, sing all the verses of "It Came Upon the Midnight Clear." Be aware of the hymn writers' references to how music played a part in creation, the incarnation, and will again on that great day of Christ's return.

Study:

When most people hear music, they can sense in their hearts that something or someone bigger than us is out there, though they may not use the word *God*. In commenting on Beethoven's Fifth Symphony, secularist Leonard Bernstein said:

> Beethoven ... turned out pieces of breathtaking rightness. Rightness—that's the word!... Our boy Beethoven has the real goods, the stuff from Heaven, the power to make you feel, at the finish: Something is right in the world. There is something that checks throughout, something that follows its own law consistently, something we can trust, something that will never let us down.[1]

There is a deep power in music, a power that connects us to the dawn of creation, to the incarnation, and to the promise of Christ's return. The first "quickening" of my spirit in childhood came through music, through hearing Beethoven's Fifth in my father's library, through hearing "O Holy Night" at a Christmas Eve candlelit church service. *Perhaps there was Someone bigger than me. Perhaps there really was a holy night when God came down.*

4. "It Came Upon the Midnight Clear" traces God's use of music from the beginning of history:

   a. *It came upon the midnight clear, that glorious song of old ...*

   How does Job 38:4–7 show this "glorious song of old" happening at creation?

   b. *And ye, beneath life's crushing load*

   What is creation doing now, and why, according to Romans 8:19–22? To what does Paul compare those groans and why? (v. 22)

c. *Peace on the earth, good will to men, from heav'n's all-gracious King! The world in solemn stillness lay to hear the angels sing.*

When did the above event happen, according to Luke 2:8–14? What hope did this give to all of cursed creation?

d. *When with the ever-circling years shall come the time foretold. . . . When the new heav'n and earth shall own the Prince of Peace their King, and the whole world send back the song which now the angels sing*

How does Isaiah 55:12–13 reflect the above lyrics? When is this?

5. Read 1 Samuel 16:14–23.

★a. What tragic thing happened, according to verse 14? How do you explain this difficult verse?

b. What did Saul's attendants understand? (vv. 15–16) Do you understand this? Explain.

★c. What request did Saul make? (v. 17) What significance do you see here that could be applicable to you in soothing your soul?

d. What did Saul's servant tell him about David, the son of Jesse? How did Saul respond to David? (vv. 18–22)

e. According to verse 23, what happened to Saul when David would play the harp? What significance do you see in this?

f. How might you apply this passage to your life? Be specific.

6. The most repeated positive phrase in Scripture is "Praise the Lord" or "Sing to the Lord." The most repeated negative command in Scripture is "Fear not" or "Do not be afraid." What connection do you see between them?

7. Ask the Lord to show you how you could better incorporate great music into your daily life. Write down what He shows you, and ask Him to tune your heart to follow through, for we can do nothing in our own strength. (Report to your group if there were any actual changes in your life musically this week and, if so, how it impacted you.)

DAY 3: THE POWER OF POETRY
("TEACH ME SOME MELODIOUS *SONNET*")

Before Beginning Your Private Study, Sing:

Try to sing the first verse of "Come Thou Fount" by heart. Sing also the first verse of "It Is Well with My Soul."

Study:

Psalms, hymns, and spiritual songs have power because they are:

- Melodious—the power of music
- Sonnets—the power of poetry
- Sung by flaming tongues above—the power of the Holy Spirit

Today we will consider the power of poetry. God uses both prose and poetry in Scripture (sometimes to recount the same event!), and each has value. Prose taps into the left side of the brain: our intellectual, reason-oriented hemisphere that longs for the facts. Poetry taps into the right side: our emotional, visually oriented hemisphere, with meter and metaphors, with sounds and scenes to penetrate the heart. Poetry can contain pages of theology in a single phrase. Its word pictures are like arrows, piercing our hearts with God's love. Prose is very clear, but poetry breaks down our walls, stays in our memory, and breathes wind in the sails of our prayer lives. However, if you attempt to interpret poetry in the same way you interpret prose, you will often misinterpret it. As C. S. Lewis says in *Reflections on the Psalms*:

> What must be said, however, is that the Psalms are poems, and poems intended to be sung:
> not doctrinal treatises, not even sermons.... Most emphatically the Psalms must be read as
> poems; as lyrics, with all the licences and all the formalities, the hyperboles, the emotional
> rather than logical connections, which are proper to lyric poetry. They must be read as poems
> if they are to be understood; no less than French must be read as French or English as English.
> Otherwise we shall miss what is in them and think we see what is not.[2]

The word *literally* actually means "according to the literature." To interpret Scripture literally, you must take into account the *kind* of literature you are reading. With prose, you can press the details, for what you have are the facts. With poetry, you may not be able to do that. For example, when the psalms talk about God riding a chariot (Psalm 18), it doesn't mean God has a body and actually rides a chariot, but rather, that He hears His child when he cries and His heart is moved toward that child. When, in Psalm 91, we are told no harm will come to the believer, we must not think that we will not suffer on earth, for that contradicts Scripture, but rather, that in the eternal scheme of things, even suffering will build character and ultimately bring good. In other words, no ultimate and lasting harm will come to the one who loves the Lord.

With poetry, look for the central meaning, contemplate the word pictures, and allow it to penetrate your heart. You are going to practice this with a few "melodious sonnets" from the psalms.

8. What did you learn about how poetry differs from prose and how that should influence your interpretation of it?

9. Read Psalm 91:1–10.

   a. What word picture in verse 4 makes it clear that this is poetry rather than prose? Explain.

   b. Meditate on this word picture in verse 4. Let it penetrate your heart. What do you see? How does it comfort you?

   c. A statement is made in verse 10 that could be misunderstood if you did not give this the license poetry requires—for harm *does* come to the believer on earth. What, therefore, does this mean? (see Romans 8:28–29 or 1 Peter 5:6–7 for a prose clarification)

   d. What would you say is the central truth of this poetic passage?

10. The following poetic word pictures from "Come Thou Fount" are based on Scripture. In each case, look up the Scripture and explain how it could have inspired Robert Robinson. Meditate on the word picture by drawing it either actually, or with words — and explain what it means to you. To meditate, you must slow down. (Look at more than one translation if possible, including the King James Version [KJV]), as that was the translation the writers of the hymns used.)

a. *Come Thou Fount of every blessing*

★(1) Jeremiah 2:13 and John 4:13

(2) Draw this word picture with figures or with words. What does it mean to you?

b. *Tune my heart to sing Thy praise*

★(1) Hebrews 13:15

(2) Draw this word picture with figures or with words. What does it mean to you?

c. *Praise the mount, I'm fixed upon it, mount of Thy redeeming love*

★(1) For "fixed upon it" see Colossians 3:1–2 and Hebrews 12:2.

(2) Draw this word picture with figures or with words. What does it mean to you?

Again sing "Come Thou Fount." Begin to learn it by heart.

DAY 4: THE POWER OF THE HOLY SPIRIT ("FLAMING TONGUES ABOVE")

There are many melodious sonnets, but what sets the psalms and Scripture-set-to-music apart is that these are the very words of God. The phrase "flaming tongues" brings to mind Pentecost —when the Holy Spirit was given, and "tongues" of fire rested on each of the believers. This God-inspired music is what can breathe life into our souls and take us into His arms. The Spirit of God gives "songs in the night."

There is a reason we are exhorted to sing "psalms, hymns, and spiritual songs." Just as different forms of literature have different purposes, so too do different kinds of music. What is fascinating, and what many believers do not realize, is that the command to sing psalms, hymns, and spiritual songs is a sub-point of another vital command.

11. Read Ephesians 5:18–21. Then note the main point in verse 18 and the three sub-points (all beginning with "S" if you use the NIV) in verses 19a, 19b, and 21.

a. Main command (v. 18b) *Be filled* _____

b. Sub-point #1 (v. 19a) *Speak* _____

c. Sub-point #2 (v. 19b) *Sing* _____

d. Sub-point #3 (v. 21) *Submit* _____

The sub-commands are evidences that the main command, that is, to be filled with the Spirit, is operating in your life. If you are filled with the Spirit, the other things will flow, the way fruit flows from a branch that is attached to the vine.

12. Are songs, thankgiving, and submission integral parts of your life? If not, what do you think is the root problem?

Music, perhaps because it is such a powerful tool against the enemy, is also a way he has sought to divide the body of Christ. The phrase "psalms, hymns, and spiritual songs"[3] has been a source of debate in the church." There was a time (and some still hold to this) when the church said that phrase simply referred to three different kinds of psalms, for it was wrong to sing anything other than Scripture verbatim in church.[4] Some churches divide into two services—a traditional service, in which they sing primarily the hymns, and a contemporary service, in which they sing primarily praise choruses—for we as believers can be quite insistent on what we think is the "best" music. I was one who used to join in with scoffers of contemporary praise choruses, calling them 7/11 songs (seven words sung eleven times). But the Lord has changed my heart, showing me we are to sing all kinds of praise to God, including the simple yet often deeply contemplative praise choruses. I remember a sermon by my pastor at that time, Mike Lano. He encouraged we who are older to submit to the younger generation, and to sing these simple praise choruses with all of our hearts. Then he encouraged those who were younger to submit to the older generation and to sing the complex hymns with all of their minds. Satan wants to divide the body of Christ, but we must overcome him by being filled with the Spirit and submitting to one another.

13. Name one of each of the following that is meaningful to you, and explain why:

   a. A psalm that is set to music: _____

   b. A hymn, rich in theological content: _____

c. A spiritual song, rich in simple contemplative phrases: _____

Sing as much as you can of "Come Thou Fount" by heart.

(Tomorrow's lesson is long, so you may want to do part of it today.)

DAY 5: EBENEZERS AND FETTERS

Before Beginning Your Private Study, Sing:

Sing verses two and three of "Come Thou Fount."

Study:

Here I Raise My Ebenezer

Some versions of "Come Thou Fount" have changed the phrase "Here I raise my Ebenezer" to something easier to understand, such as, "Hitherto Thy love has blest me." But if you know the scriptural story behind "Here I raise my Ebenezer," the word picture has much more power to stay in your heart and transform your suffering than does the substituted phrase.

First, we need to look at the historical context of this story, in which the ark of the covenant plays a prominent part. This ark was a portable chest that God had commanded Moses to build. As the ark accompanied the Israelites on their sojourn through the wilderness, they came to identify it with the presence of God.

14. Read Numbers 10:33–36.

    a. Where was the ark of the covenant as the Israelites traveled? (v. 33)

    b. What visible sign was over the Israelites and the ark? (v. 34)

    c. Describe the "song" that Moses sang as they traveled with the ark. (v. 35)

The ark of the covenant, which represented the presence and the glory of God, had a power that both the Israelites and its enemy nations recognized. The many stories of the ark in the Old Testament repeatedly are the story of the gospel, revealing first how great is the gap between us and a holy God. When people did not revere the ark, when they tried to "use" it to get blessings, great destruction came to them. But when they humbled themselves before God, the presence of the ark brought joy, peace, dancing, and blessings, demonstrating the mercy of a forgiving and loving God.

In the following account, the Philistines, desirous of the ark's blessings, capture it and bring it before their stone god, Dagon.

15. Read 1 Samuel 5:1–10.

a. What happened to the stone god Dagon the first morning? (v. 3) The second morning? (v. 4)

b. What else happened to the people there, and how did they respond? (vv. 5–8)

c. What happened in the next city to which the ark was moved? (v. 9) And then what happened in Ekron? (vv. 10–12)

d. Does the presence of the Lord always mean blessing? Explain.

16. Read 1 Samuel 7:2−9.

    a. What turning do you see in verse 2?

    b. What did Samuel tell the Israelites to do, and how did they respond? (vv. 3−4)

    c. What other evidences of a repentant heart do you see in verses 5−8?

    d. What did Samuel do in verse 9?

17. Read 1 Samuel 7:10−13.

    a. What happened when the Philistines drew near to engage Israel in battle? (vv. 10−11)

b. What stone did Samuel erect and what did he name it?

Ebenezer means "stone of help."

c. Why did the presence of the ark now bring mercy and help?

The Bible is not a series of disconnected stories, but one story. Our continuing problem is that we turn for help to things other than God. God longs to be with His children, but we have historically quenched His Spirit by seeing Him not as the *only hope*, but as *one* of our hopes. Here God's people put away their false sources of help, repented wholeheartedly with confession and fasting, and Samuel interceded and sacrificed a lamb. Today Christ is our Intercessor and our Sacrificial Lamb. He longs for us to put away our false sources of help, come to Him in repentance, and trust in Him alone. This is the gospel. The gospel reveals how bad we are (for He had to die) but how loved we are (for He did die). He is our help, our Ebenezer. His presence, like the presence of the ark when hearts are right, leads to joy, peace, and blessings.

18. What do you tend to trust in instead of God? Has suffering helped you to release this false object of trust? Explain. (Go around your circle asking for brief answers and giving people the freedom to pass.)

19. The stone Samuel set up and named Ebenezer was to help the Israelites remember God's mercy. We too can find ways to remind ourselves of God's mercy. Have you done any of the following? If so, evaluate how helpful each has been in reminding you of God's mercy.

a. A journal with answered prayers

b. A wall hanging such as a cross, a painting, or a verse

c. A piece of jewelry—a cross, a fish, etc.

d. A scrapbook with pictures and stories of ways He has worked in your life and in your family

e. Other (explain)

20. Why is it particularly important to "raise our Ebenezers" in times of trouble?

Let That Grace Now Like a Fetter

Scripture says that we are all slaves—we are all "fettered"—to something. Even after we become believers, we need to continually be set free from idols of the heart: ambition, wealth, the praise of man, gluttony, sexual immorality, and so on. Or we may be in bondage to anger against someone who has wronged us. The lyrics in "Come Thou Fount" are truly a wise, powerful, scriptural prayer that we need to sing with all of our hearts, minds, and souls to the One who can change us.

Sing the third verse of "Come Thou Fount" as a prayer, and then contemplate this particular word picture:

> Let that grace now like a fetter,
> Bind my wandering heart to Thee.

21. Look up the word *fetter* online or in a dictionary. What does it mean?

22. Read Romans 6:16–18.

    a. In verse 16, what does Paul tell us?

    ★b. Give an example of being "a slave to the one you obey" from your own life. How has it led to a kind of death?

c. Draw a fetter chaining you to whatever it is you have a tendency to obey (the call of the refrigerator, the mall, the Internet, the praise of man, etc.).

> When we obey sin instead of God, it is often because we have believed Satan's lie that God does not have our best interests at heart.

23. Meditate on 1 Peter 2:24–25.

a. What price did Jesus pay to set us free from slavery to sin?

*b. In addition to paying the price to forgive us, what else did His death on the cross make possible, according to the second part of verse 24?

c. How does Peter describe our former state in verse 25? What do you know about sheep?

Sheep are too stupid to help themselves. They do not even want to be found when they are in trouble. The shepherd has to seize the wandering sheep, throw it over his shoulders, and hold its legs firmly as it bleats in protest. We are like this. Yet Christ seeks us out, not only in salvation from hell, but in salvation from the false gods to whom we tend to enslave ourselves. Pray for your heart to respond to His grace and to abandon yourself to His goodness. What Scripture tells us is that when we yield to God's Spirit, to God's light and love, to God's still small voice—a miracle happens, for that grace actually grows stronger, binding our "wandering heart" to Him! John Stott explains it like this:

> Our love and our hatred not only reveal if we are in the light or the darkness, but actually contribute to the light or darkness in which we already are.[5]

And Paul puts it like this:

> You are slaves to the one you obey—whether you are slaves to sin, which leads to death, or to obedience, which leads to righteousness.
>
> ROMANS 6:16b

> Just as you used to offer the parts of your body in slavery to impurity and to ever-increasing wickedness, so now offer them in slavery to righteousness leading to holiness.
>
> ROMANS 6:19b

Do not think that Paul is saying that we can, in our own strength, become holy. We will fail every day. But as we gaze on what Jesus did for us, as we understand the gospel more and more, the fetters which bound us to sin will be broken, and they will instead bind us to Him. He will change our hearts of stone to hearts of flesh.

24. If you read chapter 3 of the book *The God of All Comfort*, what stood out to you?

25. What do you think you will remember from this study? Why?

GROUP PRAYER TIME

Circle in groups of three and four for conversational prayer, opening to the lyrics of "Come Thou Fount." Have someone read a few lines, using that as a springboard for conversational prayer. Then continue like that, through the song.

O the Deep, Deep Love of Jesus*

O the deep, deep love of Jesus,
Vast, unmeasured, boundless, free!
Rolling as a mighty ocean
In its fullness over me!
Underneath me, all around me,
Is the current of Thy love
Leading onward, leading homeward
To Thy glorious rest above!

O the deep, deep love of Jesus,
Spread His praise from shore to shore!
How He loveth, ever loveth;
Changeth never, nevermore!
How He watches o'er His loved ones
Died to call them all His own;
How for them He intercedeth
Watcheth o'er them from the throne!

O the deep, deep love of Jesus,
Love of every love the best!
'Tis an ocean vast of blessing,
'Tis a haven sweet of rest!
O the deep, deep love of Jesus,
'Tis a heaven of heavens to me;
And it lifts me up to glory,
For it lifts me up to Thee!

WORDS BY: S. TREVOR FRANCIS, 1875
MUSIC BY: THOMAS J. WILLIAMS, 1890
ARR. BY: AMY S. WIXTROM AND GARY WIXTROM, 2001
©2002 G. B. WIX PUBLISHING ASCAP

* Available on the companion music CD

DEEP CALLS TO DEEP

(Hymn: "O the Deep, Deep Love of Jesus")

THE HYMN "O THE DEEP, DEEP LOVE OF JESUS" (HEREAFTER SHORTENED TO "DEEP, DEEP LOVE") is as much an emotional experience as an intellectual one. This week you will immerse yourself in the water metaphors of the Psalter and taste, see, feel, and hear how they convey the love, nourishment, and power of God.

The academic left-brained approach to the psalms—focusing on their structure, genre, and style—is certainly not without value. By itself, however, it can rip the heart out of a psalm, leaving the Psalter dead on the operating table. When Luci Shaw's daughter dissected a grasshopper in high school biology she said, with disgust, "As if that's any way to know a grasshopper."[1] We must see the psalm pictures alive and whole, leaping into our hearts, transforming our souls. In *Seeing the Psalms*, William P. Brown explains that scholars have overlooked the imagery of the psalms "at great theological cost." The psalms, he explains, "find their relevance primarily in what they evoke rather than in the countless ways they can be dissected and categorized."[2]

ICEBREAKER

Think of a time when water was a welcome relief to you: a refreshing lake, a comforting Jacuzzi, a longed-for rain, or a tall drink of water. What is your specific memory? What were your feelings?

DAY 1: LORD OF THE STORM

Water images flow through the Psalter. In the first lesson we saw how the psalmist uses pictures of drowning to convey his desperate need for the Lord's rescue, how sea billows can convey sorrow, and how a river can convey peace. In all water images, positive or negative, God is in control. He is enthroned over the flood; He is Lord of the wind and the waves.

As you look at the water images in the Psalter, slow down and allow them to surround your senses, the way you would slow down before a great painting by Rembrandt or Monet in the Louvre. If you whiz by, you'll miss the message, the meaning, and the memorable kiss of God.

The first picture, found in Psalm 29, is a furious storm. Imagine that you are at the beach. Clouds begin to move in and a dead calm comes over the bay. The sky darkens and lightning flashes in the distance. You hear a low growl of thunder and join the other sunbathers who are quickly grabbing their things and making a run for it. As you run, the lightning cracks, and you jump. The sky opens up, pelting you with huge, hard drops. Ducking into your beach cabin, you wrap yourself in a blanket, unable to take your eyes from the scene outside. The breakers are enormous, the thunder rolls, and occasionally the darkened scene is completely illuminated by jagged bolts. Words of "How Great Thou Art" come to mind, as you think about the Lord of the Storm.

Before Beginning Your Private Study, Sing:

Sing the first verse of "How Great Thou Art" (available at cyberhymnal.org, or Google it). Then listen to Amy sing "Deep, Deep Love" on the companion CD and sing along.

Study:

1. Read Psalm 29 slowly, picturing yourself in the scene, taking in the images with your senses.

    a. What are David's initial thoughts as he watches this gathering storm? (vv. 1–2)

    b. What are some ways you might "hear" a storm?

c. What are some ways the psalmist hears the storm? Give verse references and then describe what he hears.

★d. What important fact do you find in verse 10? What does this mean?

★e. What other important fact do you find about the Lord of the Storm in verse 11?

2. Read Mark 4:35–41.

a. Describe the storm that caused these experienced fishermen such fear. Look carefully at verse 37 and find everything you can to describe the ferocity of this storm.

b. What feelings are expressed by the disciples in verse 38? Have you ever felt that way about the Lord? Explain.

c. Satan always wants us to believe that God doesn't care, doesn't love us. If we believe that, how does that influence us in the storms of life?

d. What does Jesus do, and what happens as a result? (v. 39)

> Pastor Tim Keller says that all religions believe that only God can control the sea. This is clear in the historical account of Jonah, where all the sailors were each calling on their own god. When any man tried to calm the sea, it was always in the name of his "higher power." But Jesus is God, and calls upon no one. He simply says, in the Greek, "Be still and stay still." And it does.[3]

e. What question did the disciples ask in verse 41? How did they feel? Why do you think they felt that way?

3. No doubt purposely, Mark uses parallel language to that of Jonah's story. Find the parallels between these two historical accounts:

a. Jonah 1:4   Mark 4:37

b. Jonah 1:5–6   Mark 4:38

c. Jonah 1:15–16   Mark 4:39–41

4. Why did Jonah have to be thrown into the storm of the ocean? (Jonah 1:8–12)

5. Why did Jesus have to be thrown into the storm of the crucifixion? How does Jesus describe this pit in Matthew 12:40?

*6. What differences do you see between the hearts of Jonah and Jesus? What should this tell us in the storms of life?

Learn the first verse of "Deep, Deep Love."

DAY 2: STREAMS OF WATER

"Deep, Deep Love" became one of the main hymns I sang as the waters of grief began to subside. By the third year after Steve's death, though I still wept daily, I also was sensing more of the presence of God. Three dear sisters in Christ who had stood by me in my grief came to the cabin for a long weekend. I remember sitting in the Jacuzzi with them, watching the sun set over Green Bay, and singing "Deep, Deep Love" as the water swirled about us:

Underneath me, all around me, is the current of His love ...

In Psalm 42, there are four water pictures, beginning with a dry riverbed. However, by the end of the psalm, the dry riverbed is *charged* with water, or, as William Brown puts it, transformed "from a silent, barren wadi to the thunderous roar of flood-borne waves."[4]

Today we'll look at the "rivers of water," the metaphor for the Spirit of God, the presence of God within us. This is what the psalmist longs for in Psalm 42, but he is as disappointed as the thirsty panting deer that has made its way all the way down the mountain to the river, only to find it dry. Those who have experienced deep loss can identify. Though you need to be comforted, your soul refuses to be comforted. Though you are thirsty, it seems the riverbed is dry. You wonder, *Where are you, God?* After Steve died, I knew in my head that God was good and loving, but I certainly wasn't sensing that love "underneath me, all around me."

This opening water picture of "streams of water" represents the nourishment that the presence of God brings. As the rain revives the earth, as streams of water revive the deer, so it is that God's Spirit quickens us.

Before You Begin Your Private Study, Sing:

Sing "As the Deer," if you know it (available on iTunes, or Google it), and "Deep, Deep Love."

Study:

7. In Psalm 1:2–3, to what is the godly man compared? What do you think the "streams of water" represent?

8. What is Isaiah's call in Isaiah 55:1–3? What do you learn about this water, this food?

9. Read Hosea 6:1–3.

   a. What is Hosea's call and promise in verses 1–2?

   b. Describe the metaphor in verse 3.

10. Read John 4:13–14. What do you learn about the water that Jesus gives?

11. How have you experienced this living water that revives? Share a recent experience, if possible.

12. Read Psalm 42, noting below repeated phrases, cries of lament, and overall emotion.

13. What water picture do you find in Psalm 42:1? Parallelism is the main way the psalms communicate feelings. What is the parallel here? What does this tell you about how the psalmist is feeling?

14. Share a time when you longed for the presence of God, sought after Him, but did not sense Him.

Sing the first verse of "Deep, Deep Love" by heart.

DAY 3: TEARS DAY AND NIGHT

The psalmist is longing for streams of water, but he says the only water he is getting is his "tears … day and night" (Psalm 42:3). If you look carefully at the psalmist's description of himself, you will see evidence of clinical depression, an important topic for all of us to understand. We will also look at some other key passages on tears, learning the difference between sweet tears and bitter tears, and what it means that the Lord says He collects all our tears in a bottle.

★15. Read Psalm 42:3–4 to discern the symptoms of depression the psalmist experienced.

a. What has been his food? What does this tell you about his eating habits?

b. What do you learn about his sleeping?

c. What do you learn about his fellowship with other believers?

Just as human beings are complicated, so depression is complicated. The most effective solutions take in the whole person: physical, spiritual, and emotional. To ignore any of these spheres could easily lead to failure in overcoming depression.

Physical Aspects:

Often what keeps us from good health habits of sleeping, eating, and exercising properly is anxiety. We lay awake, worrying. We either stop eating, or grab unhealthy, fast "comfort" foods instead of preparing meals that will restore our bodies. We feel too sluggish to exercise. Because our body is being abused from these poor habits, we spiral deeper into depression. The following passages, therefore, address the root problem.

16. Read Matthew 6:24–34.

a. What statement does Jesus make in verse 24? What is His reasoning?

b. How does He elaborate on the above reasoning in verse 25?

c. What reason does He give in verse 26 for not worrying about money, food, or clothing?

d. What other reason does He give for not worrying in verse 27?

e. What second example does He give in verses 28–29?

f. What promise is given in verse 33?

Read Matthew 6:34 in the following paraphrase:

Give your entire attention to what God is doing right now, and don't get worked up about what may or may not happen tomorrow. God will help you deal with whatever hard things come up when the time comes.

Matthew 6:34 (MSG)

This verse is one I memorized when Steve was ill. Anxieties multiplied as I thought about what life would be like in days ahead if the Lord didn't heal him on earth. This verse helped me take a day at a time and to trust God for the hard days ahead. And when Steve *did* die, it helped me again. In the night, I often give my worries to the Lord as an act of worship, showing Him I do trust Him to help me deal with these things.

g. How could you apply verse 34 to your life right now?

Many individuals battling depression have a chemical imbalance, as real as the imbalance that a diabetic has. Though most Christians would not stop a diabetic from getting insulin, they often do stand in the way of a depressed person getting help to correct his or her chemical imbalance. A high percentage of suicides are a result of this untreated chemical imbalance. Jesus said, "The sick need a physician."

Emotional Aspects:

In Psalm 42, the psalmist is isolated—probably not by choice but by circumstance, but his isolation contributes to his depression. We are emotional beings designed for fellowship with God and with one another.

17. Read Ecclesiastes 4:9–12.

a. What are some reasons "two are better than one"?

b. What do you think a "cord of three strands" could mean?

c. Are you proactive about staying in Christian fellowship with others? What do you do together?

The psalmist often uses the picture of "sinking in the mire." When you are going down in quicksand, the more you struggle, the deeper you go. What you need is a helping hand to pull you out. A Christian counselor can be truly used of God to be that hand. (Two excellent Internet resources to help you find a counselor in your area are the American Association of Christian Counselors [www.aacc.net/] and Focus on the Family [www.family.org or www.focusonthefamily.com].)

When Steve was ill, I often lay awake sobbing, keeping him awake as well. Though I resisted, I finally went to see my internist who put me on an anti-anxiety medicine. When I was then able to sleep, I was also better able to be the support Steve needed.

Spiritual Aspects:

Sometimes our depression exists because there is a sin to repent of, and we must do that to have our burden released. Sometimes we have not sinned, but are under spiritual attack. We have an enemy who is on the prowl, looking for those who have been weakened by storms and are therefore especially vulnerable to his lies.

18. What is the repeated taunt in Psalm 42:3b and 42:10b?

> Satan is continually trying to cause "attachment disorder" between the children of God and God, whispering to us that the One who should have protected us has abandoned us. When Satan attacked Jesus, Jesus responded with Scripture.

19. What does Hebrews 13:5c say?

Because Jesus was forsaken on the cross, we know we never will be. Satan lies to us, telling us the Lord doesn't care, but Scripture repeatedly tells us the reverse. Meditate on the following image:

> You keep track of all my sorrows.
> You have collected all my tears in your bottle.
> You have recorded each one in your book.
> PSALM 56:8 (NLT)

The above image is particularly meaningful if your tears are "bitter ones." I lost a dear husband, so my tears are "sweet tears." So many women have told me to count my blessings, for their marriages ended because of betrayal, abuse, or abandonment. Their tears are bitter tears. William Brown explains that the Psalm 56 image of the bottle or flask holding tears is significant, in that "God is exhorted, albeit indirectly, to drink the full measure of the psalmist's tears to ensure that his grievances will not be passed over but duly digested and, thus, recorded."[5] Knowing that God, the perfect Judge, will deal with those who hurt you may help you to forgive. Forgiveness is another significant factor to emotional health, for it purges the poison of anger that can otherwise destroy us.

20. Do you have "bitter tears"? Have you been able to forgive? Why is it important that you ask God to give you the grace to do so?

Memorize the second verse of "Deep, Deep Love" and be ready to sing it when Satan tries to make you question God's love.

DAY 4: DEEP CALLS TO DEEP

Study:

The next image of water in Psalm 42 is of a waterfall. Here is the psalmist, parched and thirsty, yet now, in the distance, he hears the deep echoing thunder of a waterfall. What does this mean, this "deep calling to deep"? Understood rightly, this passage will minister deep into your soul.

21. The key to understanding verse 7 is in verses 5–6. One "deep" is the soul. How is she described in verse 5?

The other "deep" is the One who can catch us. Explaining "deep calls to deep," the great seventeenth-century author John Bunyan wrote, "What's that? Why, it is expressed in the verse before. 'O God,' says he, 'my soul is cast down within me.' 'Down' that is deep into the jaws of distrust and fear … Like falling into a well or dungeon … Do, of thy compassions, open those everlasting arms, and catch him that has no help or stay in himself."[6]

Likewise, Corrie Ten Boom, and her sister, Betsy, in the midst of the deep pain of the Nazis' Rävensbrück concentration camp, said: "There is no pit so deep that God's love is not deeper still."

I have also thought of it as the deep voice of God speaking deep into my downcast soul.

There have been times in my life when my soul is so fretful that I feel like I'm drowning, as in Psalm 18, when the psalmist cried that "the cords of death were entangling him." Yet God has come running, reaching down, "drawing [me] out of deep waters." I have seen Him come running to my children as well. On my youngest daughter's wedding day, she came down the stairs tearful that morning, missing her dad, asking: "Do you think Dad can see?"

Trying to comfort her, I said, "I think he can. I think that's what the 'great cloud of witnesses' in Hebrews 12 is about."

"But you can't be absolutely sure, can you?"

"No, I guess I can't."

"Do you think he'd be excited for me today?"

"Oh, yes. He'd love David."

"But you can't be positive, can you?"

At that moment our son, Annie's older brother, came running in with one of Steve's Bibles. "Look, Annie—look at this sticky note that was in the front of Dad's Bible."

We both looked.

Dear Annie

I love you so much.
I am so excited for you.
Dad

Deep calls to deep. Out of the deep waters. The deep voice of God deep into Annie's soul.

22. If possible, share a time when "deep called to deep."

Sing the first two verses of "Deep, Deep Love" by heart.

DAY 5: WAVES AND BREAKERS

The fourth and final water picture in Psalm 42 occurs in verse 7b, when the psalmist says, "All your waves and breakers have swept over me." For me, water is almost always a positive image. I grew up playing in the waves, swimming through them and underneath them. I still love swimming under water—the clamorous world completely silenced; my whole body gently caressed; and an unseen world opened to me as I view, especially in tropical waters, swarms of fish without number in iridescent electrifying colors. Yet I realize not everybody feels as I do about being surrounded by water. When my husband, Steve, and I came home from Hawaii, I said, "My absolute high point of the trip was snorkeling. What was yours?"

Quite seriously, Steve responded, "My high point was not drowning."

Here, the images of "waves and breakers" sweeping over you may sound negative, but if you look at it in the context of the whole psalm, there's an important change.

23. In the second water image, that of tears, find the "day and night" image. (v. 3) How is it negative here?

24. Now, look at the "day and night" image in verse 8 that follows "waves and breakers." How is it positive? How does this reverse the negative image of verse 3?

25. The beginning of the psalm pictured a dry riverbed. In contrast, what is pictured now? (v. 7)

26. Meditate on the third verse of "Deep, Deep Love." How are the water images positive?

27. If you read chapter 4 of the book *The God of All Comfort*, what stood out to you?

28. What do you think you will remember about this week's lesson and why?

Sing "Deep, Deep Love." If you know Matt Redman's song, "All Who Are Thirsty" (available on iTunes, or Google it), sing it as well. It likewise describes the water pictures of Psalm 42.

Group Prayer Time

Begin with a time of praise, lifting up with thanksgiving your answers to question 16 (page 76). Then continue by lifting up a deep need in your life, and let the others support you in sentence prayers. Close together by singing the first verse of "Deep, Deep Love."

Be Thou My Vision*

Be Thou my vision, O Lord of my heart;
Naught be all else to me, save that Thou art.
Thou my best thought, by day or by night,
Waking or sleeping, Thy presence my light.

Riches I heed not, nor man's empty praise,
Thou mine inheritance, now and always:
Thou and Thou only, first in my heart,
High king of heaven, my treasure Thou art.

High king of heaven, my victory won,
May I reach heaven's joys, O bright heaven's Sun!
Heart of my own heart, whatever befall,
Still be my vision, O ruler of all

Words attributed to: Dallan Forgaill, 8th century
Translated from ancient Irish to English by: Mary E. Byrne, 1905
Versed by Eleanor H. Hull, 1912
Music by: Irish folk origin in the Slane Hill, County of Meathe
Arr. by: Amy S. Wixtrom and Gary Wixtrom, 1995 and 2009
©1995 G. B. Wix Publishing ASCAP

*Available on the companion music CD

WHY ARE YOU DOWNCAST, O MY SOUL?

(Hymn: "Be Thou My Vision")

IN PSALM 42 AND PSALM 43, THE PSALMIST ANALYZES WHERE HE HAS PLACED HIS HOPE, repeatedly asking this question of his soul:

> Why are you downcast, O my soul?
> Why so disturbed [disquieted, NKJV] within me?
>
> PSALM 42:5, 11; 43:5

He is asking, "*Why,* truly, *did* I get so downcast?" He is analyzing where his hope lies.

Most of us have a "default setting" where we automatically turn for hope and security instead of God. Usually it is a good thing, which is what makes it deceptive. *Why would this be wrong?* we wonder. *Isn't family, or ministry, or comfort a good thing?* But we've made a good thing an ultimate thing. We've become idolaters. We've "run after other gods." And unless we stop and listen to our souls, our sorrows will increase.[1]

ICEBREAKER

In this study, we are going to study how to listen to our souls. Listening is an art. Think about both a good listener and a bad listener. What are some of the differences?

DAY 1: WHEN THE LORD SHAKES OUR WORLD

Before Beginning Your Private Study, Sing:

Using the CD, sing "Be Thou My Vision" along with Amy in your private quiet time.

Study:

Twice in Psalm 42 and once in Psalm 43, the psalmist asks his soul the same question:

Why are you downcast, O my soul?

Painful times can result in a sharp learning curve, because our world has been shaken, and that shaking has revealed that something (or someone) other than God has been our foundation, "our vision," the source of our hope. In Psalm 42, when the psalmist's world has been shaken, he wisely takes his soul in hand and asks her, "Why are you downcast?" He is trying to identify her false source of hope and redirect her hope to God, who can never be shaken.

1. In Psalm 42–43, each time the psalmist asks the question, "Why are you downcast, O my soul?" what exhortation follows?

★2. What similar thought can you find in the lyrics of "Be Thou My Vision"?

David was a man after God's heart, not because he never trusted in a false source of hope, but because he was teachable. Whenever God would shake his world, David would listen, though sometimes God had to speak to him more than once. But eventually David would hear, repent, and redirect his soul to trust in God.

Later in David's life, his son Absalom led a revolt against him, trying to seize the kingdom. David's men thwarted the coup, but as a result, Absalom died. Despite the fact that Absalom had betrayed him, David was shattered.

3. Read 2 Samuel 18:31–33.

   a. What news did the Cushite bring to David, and what was David's first question?

   b. How did the Cushite respond?

   c. Find everything you can about David's reaction in verse 33.

   d. How is David's response understandable?

   e. How does David's response also reveal a wrong perspective?

4. Read 2 Samuel 19:1–8.

   a. How did Joab rebuke David in verses 5–6?

b. What did Joab ask David to do in verse 7?

c. How did David respond?

The following are warning signs that you have allowed a person to become what only Jesus should be:

- You think about this person obsessively—whenever your mind is at rest.
- You feel that if they were not in your life you would not be able to go on.
- You are anxious if you cannot spend frequent and exclusive time with this person. (The exception would be a spouse—but even then, we should be able to give our spouse freedom to do things that may not include us.)

Do you have any of the above warning signs concerning a person?

5. What is the difference between cherishing our spouses, our children, and our friends and making them our "Solid Rock"?

6. Many of David's psalms show him talking to his soul, redirecting her to trust only in God. Psalm 3 was written "when David fled from his son Absalom." Read it. What phrases show you that David is redirecting his hope to God?

★7. What do the following lyrics mean?

> Be Thou my vision, O Lord of my heart
> Naught be all else to me, save that Thou art.

8. Think of a time when your world was shaken, as was David's. If you had listened to your soul, what might you have learned about where she was misplacing her hope? How might it have been an understandable and yet dangerous perspective?

Sing "Be Thou My Vision" as a prayer.

DAY 2: HEALING OF SPIRITUAL VISION IS A PROCESS

Before Beginning Your Private Study, Sing:

Memorize the first verse of "Be Thou My Vision" and then sing it to the Lord as a prayer in your private quiet time.

Study:

When I was a young woman, my dream was to get thin, snare a wonderful husband, have beautiful children, and live in a house overlooking the ocean. Such was my vision for meaning and purpose in life. I got them all, but they didn't satisfy the emptiness in me. I was the feminine counterpart of the preacher in Ecclesiastes, who, after he got everything he thought he wanted, cried: "Meaningless, meaningless. My life is meaningless." My soul was downcast, and I couldn't understand why.

But Jesus did not leave me. He sent someone—my sister—to speak the truth to my soul, so that He could touch me and help me see. He changed my vision. But as is true of all of us, our vision cannot be completely changed with one touch. Today we will study a miracle that is unique because it is the only one where Jesus healed in stages. It teaches a vital truth.

9. For an overview, read Mark 8:22–26 and describe what happened in this incident.

10. What miracle did Jesus perform in Mark 8:1–13?

11. Read Mark 8:14–21.

   a. What had the disciples forgotten to bring, according to verse 14?

   b. What warning does Jesus give them in verse 15?

   ★c. What do you think the "yeast" of the Pharisees is?

   d. What do the disciples think Jesus is talking about?

   e. What does Jesus say to them in verses 17–18?

f. What does He remind them of in verses 19–20?

g. What question does He ask in verse 21?

It is almost humorous that the disciples are so focused on having enough bread, considering the miracle that has just happened. But the main point here is that we all focus on earthly things when Jesus wants to be our focus, our vision, our life. When He tells the disciples to beware of the yeast of the Pharisees, He is warning them about the Pharisee's erroneous teaching: believing they could save themselves by keeping the Law.

In the same way, we often look to other things besides Jesus to be our vision, to be our way of finding meaning and security in life. Even when we come to Christ, as the disciples had, we need Him to continually touch us to be healed of our spiritual blindness. We must beware of the yeast in the world that tells us that beauty, possessions, fame, or even morality is what gives us purpose and security. This miracle, which we will now study, is bracketed on the other side by Jesus' question to Peter: "Who do you say that I am?" Only Jesus can be our vision. "Naught be all else," or, "nothing else will do."

12. Read the miracle again in Mark 8:22–26.

   a. How, according to verse 22, were friends involved in this healing? How can you tell they were truly friends?

   b. How have true friends been involved in getting you to Jesus to receive spiritual vision? Share one specific example.

> We will return to this thought on Days 4 and 5,
> for spiritual blindness is often healed in community.

c. What did Jesus do, and what question did He ask in verse 23?

d. What was the man's response? (v. 24)

⋆e. This is the only miracle where Jesus healed in stages. What do you think is the significance of this?

⋆f. What spiritual parallel might there be to "seeing men as trees walking"?

My dear son-in-law, David, who loves the Lord deeply and has such a heart for people, tells me this image describes him as a teenager, even though he was a believer at the time. "I didn't really see people, because I was so absorbed in myself. I saw them as 'trees walking.'"

13. Our souls can be enlarged through loss if we do not back away from God. Often it is then that we receive another touch, refocus, and make Jesus our vision, our Rock. Think about a time of loss where you also grew spiritually. What happened, and how did your vision change?

Memorize the first six lines of "Be Thou My Vision."

DAY 3: UNDERSTANDING PARALLELISM IN PSALMS AND HYMNS

Before Beginning Your Private Study, Sing:

Memorize the second verse of "Be Thou My Vision" and then sing it to the Lord as a prayer in your private quiet time.

Study:

Parallelism is the most common pattern in the psalms, and also in many hymns. It is simply saying the same thing twice in different words. For example:

> The One enthroned in heaven laughs;
> the Lord scoffs at them.
>
> PSALM 2:4

> Those who look to him are radiant;
> their faces are never covered with shame.
>
> PSALM 34:5

Parallelism is a helpful device, for if you don't understand the first line, the second helps to explain it. The same device is common in hymns. For example:

> Here I raise my Ebenezer;
> Hither by Thy help I'm come.

Parallelism provides context, and context aids in correct interpretation. Just as it is vital to read Scripture in context, we must look at the context of hymns. "Be Thou My Vision" is a clear example. A repeated thought in Scripture is that it isn't sufficient to turn away from false gods, such as riches or people, but we absolutely must allow the Lord to fill our hearts. If we don't, we will, in our emptiness and blindness, simply turn to a different false god.

The first picture in each verse of "Be Thou My Vision" concludes with a complementary picture as the verse closes (note the two underlined phrases in verse one below):

> <u>Be Thou my vision</u>, O Lord of my heart;
> Naught be all else to me, save that Thou art.
> Thou my best thought, by day or by night.
> Waking or sleeping, <u>Thy presence my light</u>.

★14. Meditate on the connection between vision and light in the first verse, between the plea and the answer. What do you see?

★15. Now, underline and connect the complementary opening and closing in the second verse. Explain how they go together.

> Riches I heed not, nor man's empty praise,
> Thou mine inheritance, now and always;
> Thou and Thou only, first in my heart,
> High king of heaven, my treasure Thou art.

★16. Underline and connect the complementary opening and closing in the third verse. Explain how they go together.

> High king of heaven, my victory won,
> May I reach heaven's joys, O bright heaven's Sun!
> Heart of my own heart, whatever befall,
> Still be my vision, O ruler of all!

17. How is God speaking to you through your contemplations on "Be Thou My Vision"?

DAY 4: HEALING OF SPIRITUAL VISION OFTEN HAPPENS IN COMMUNITY

Before Beginning Your Private Study, Sing:

Sing the first and second verses of "Be Thou My Vision" with your mind, and by heart!

Study:

The friends of the blind man in Mark 8 brought him to Jesus and begged Jesus to heal him. This is such a beautiful picture of the value of Christianity community. We need each other for many reasons, but one important reason is that someone else in the body of Christ may be able to see what we cannot. Our depravity is strong, our darkness deep, and our enemy intent on blinding us. A true friend may bring the light we desperately need. Here are just a few testimonies I've heard:

- I couldn't see that I had a pattern of clinging too tightly to a friend. I remember when I was in a friendship with one woman and she got a boyfriend, I felt physically ill. My other friends saw it—and one in particular gave me the name of a good Christian counselor. That counselor turned the light on for me by naming my sin: "relational idolatry." It took time and work, but the truth has set me free. My friendships are healthy and life-giving now. (Christy)

- I couldn't see how heavy I had gotten. When I looked in the mirror, I didn't look that bad. But when my friend put pictures she'd taken of me on Facebook it was a real wake-up call. I did your study, *A Woman of Moderation*, and have lost thirty-five pounds. (Selena)

- I really thought the problem in my marriage was my husband, and I was increasingly angry with him. But when I prayed about it with a friend, she prayed so hard for him because of the enormous stress he was under. Suddenly I realized there were two people hurting in our marriage, and my attitude began to change. And that made his attitude change toward me. I can hardly believe how good our marriage is today. (Meredith)

18. Can you think of one time a friend, a counselor, or the body of Christ brought light to your darkness? Share briefly.

19. What contributing factors can you find for spiritual blindness in the following Scriptures?

    a. 2 Corinthians 4:4

    b. Matthew 15:14

    c. 1 John 2:9–11

20. We must not underestimate how sin can lead to increasing blindness. This can be seen in the progressive sin of David, who first committed adultery and then murdered—and still couldn't see. How did God use a friend to bring light to him, according to 2 Samuel 12:1–13?

Nathan used a word picture which can sometimes penetrate better than accusations or didactic Scriptures. For example, instead of saying, "You don't have scriptural reasons to get a divorce," it might be more effective to say "What do you think your life will be like ten years after your divorce? What will Christmas be like? How will you feel about family photo albums?" Or, instead of "You shouldn't get an abortion," you might ask "Do you think your baby is a boy or a girl? Do you think she might be like you?"

21. The stronger our friends, the more light they have, the more helped we will be by being in community with them. The book of Proverbs tells us to "be cautious in friendship," and is filled with exhortations on how to evaluate character. (Proverbs use parallelism as well, sometimes with a complementary thought and sometimes with a contrast.) Find the characteristic of a strong friend in each of the following:

a. Proverbs 20:6

b. Proverbs 27:6

c. Proverbs 27:9

22. Spend some private time in prayer, asking the Lord to shine light into the strength of your community. Do you have strong Christian friends? Are you in a strong church, a strong small group? Do your closest friends sharpen you, and you them? Be still and hear from the Lord.

DAY 5: THE VALUE OF CHRISTIAN COUNSELORS

Often spiritual healing can happen through our brothers and sisters in Christ. A strong brother or sister is, according to Romans 15:14, competent to advise. But there are also times when people need expertise their friends are not likely to have. We really may be over our head when dealing with a friend's or family member's obsessive-compulsive disorder, addictions, suicidal depression, or high-tide grief. And if we are the one who is overwhelmed with any of these issues, we may resist getting help. A wise friend will encourage us to get it—even go with us the first time.

After Steve died, I resisted getting help. Why? In part, it was pride—I thought I was mature enough to do this alone. I didn't want to go to the GriefShare groups that a friend kept inviting me to because I thought, *I'm one of the speakers on that GriefShare video—I can't go!* (GriefShare is an excellent support group, and if you live in a city it is likely you can find a nearby meeting through the Internet.) The *other* part of my problem, though, was denial. Now I realize that I resisted help because if I went for help it meant Steve had really died. Denial, as wild as it sounds, is real.

Joan Didion titled the book she wrote after her husband's sudden death, *The Year of Magical Thinking.* Though it may seem crazy to others, those who are experiencing enormous emotional pain may live in a fantasy world until they are strong enough to face reality.

Didion writes that the night of her husband's death, the doctors approached her gently about doing an autopsy. Because an autopsy is gruesome, it is often a very sensitive subject, a difficult one to broach with a spouse or a parent already reeling from the news that the one who was so precious to them has died. But Didion surprised the doctors by agreeing immediately and wholeheartedly. She thought, *If they find out what went wrong, then "they might still be able to fix it."*[2] When asked if she would donate his organs, she couldn't do that (*certainly not, if he wasn't really dead*) but simply told the doctor that their daughter didn't even know yet that her father had died. When asked to write an obituary, she again balked. (*If she wrote an obituary, people might think her husband was dead.*) And she didn't want to give away his clothes because then he wouldn't have anything to wear when he came back.

I didn't think I was in denial. I even went on Focus on the Family after Steve died and said I didn't think denial was a real phenomenon. (They wisely edited out that comment.) After a year, I realized I wasn't getting better, but perhaps worse. I finally accepted that I needed help, another voice to speak the truth to my soul.[3]

Sheila, a trained Christian counselor, was able to see things that my friends, as dear and strong in the Lord as they were, could not see.

Monday, April 10

Holy Week, a year and a half after Steve's death

I told Sheila about the dream I had the night before Sally's wedding.

I drove up to the church alone and suddenly, Steve pulled up right next to me, put his window down, and smiled that great smile.

I said, "You aren't dead!"

"Oh no," he said. "I thought you were really mad at me so I was giving you space. But I found out you weren't angry. It was all a terrible misunderstanding. I'm here. I'm alive. And I'll never go away again."

Then we hugged and wept and he walked into the church with me. I knew how thrilled Sally would be to see him, to have him walk her down the aisle.

But then I woke up. I told Sheila I wept. I wept for Sally, I wept for me, I wept for Steve.

Gently, Sheila said: "Dee—you must face the truth that Steve is not coming home as you know it. You must accept that you will not see him until you die."

Has my thinking really been that delusional?

Yes. There is a part of me that thinks that if I get through enough hard nights that then I will deserve to have him come back to me.

I am a madwoman.

When Sheila helped me to speak and listen to my soul, I could see why my soul was so disquieted. I was basing my hope, in part, on a lie. The lie, like a painful blister or boil, had to be lanced so I could get better. My hope, my confidence, had to be based on the hope I had in Christ—and not on anyone or anything else. This was a turning point for me. Instead of basing my hope on a lie, I began to speak the truth to my soul. The hymn we are going to study in the next lesson became my nightly lullaby for the next year, breathing the truth I so desperately needed for healing. And healing came.

23. What does Jeremiah 17:9 say about our hearts?

24. To what does Proverbs 20:5a compare our hearts?

25. Who can draw out the deep waters of our hearts?

26. Why might a Christian who has studied grief, suicide, addictions, etc., be a wise choice if you are struggling with one of those weights?

27. Why do we so often resist getting the help we need?

28. If you read chapter 5 of the book *The God of All Comfort,* what stood out to you?

29. What do you think you will remember about this lesson and why?

GROUP PRAYER TIME

Circle in a small group. Often we hide behind the needs of others with our prayer requests. While it is true we should intercede for others, we should also make ourselves vulnerable in trusted community. Has the Lord revealed an area of weakness in your own heart? Lift it up and let the others support you with sentence prayers. If you are not comfortable naming it, then simply say, "God has shown me a weakness in my life," and let them pray for you. Close with the first verse of "Be Thou My Vision."

Be Still, My Soul*

Be still, my soul: the Lord is on thy side.
Bear patiently the cross of grief or pain.
Leave to thy God to order and provide;
In every change, He faithful will remain.
Be still, my soul: thy best, thy heavenly Friend
Through thorny ways leads to a joyful end.

Be still, my soul: thy God doth undertake
To guide the future, as He has the past.
Thy hope, thy confidence let nothing shake;
All now mysterious shall be bright at last.
Be still, my soul: the wind and waves still know
His voice that ruled them while He dwelt below.

Be still, my soul: the hour is hastening on
When we shall be forever with the Lord.
When disappointment, grief, and fear are gone,
Sorrow forgot, love's purest joys restored.
Be still, my soul: when change and tears are past,
All safe and blessed we shall meet at last.

Words by: Katharina A. von Schlegel, 1752
Translated from German to English by: Jane L. Borthwick, 1855
Music by: Jean Sibelius, 1899 ("Finlandia")
Arr. by: Amy S. Wixtrom and Gary Wixtrom, 1997
©1998 G. B. WIX Publishing ASCAP

* Available on the companion music CD

BE STILL, MY SOUL

(Hymn: "Be Still, My Soul")

ONE HYMN COMFORTED ME MORE THAN ANY OTHER THAT SUMMER AFTER I BEGAN COUNSELING with Sheila. "Be Still, My Soul" became my nightly lullaby. I had to let go of the fraying rope of lies to which I had been clinging (that Steve might return to me) and grab the sturdy rope of truth. Three important truths are found in "Be Still, My Soul," and I latched onto them like a hungry baby latches on to his mother's breast. Every night as I sang the hymn, these truths and perfectly paired melody—the majestic national anthem, "Finlandia"—calmed and soothed my soul.

This hymn has comforted believers in pain for generations. It has come to be associated with Eric Liddell, the Olympic runner whose story and integrity were made famous in the film *Chariots of Fire*. Liddell became a missionary to China after the 1924 Olympics and was interred in a Chinese prison camp where he died of a brain tumor. Before his death he taught "Be Still, My Soul" to his fellow inmates. As with us, Liddell's rescue was a different kind of rescue, but it was a real rescue. On the afternoon of Liddell's death, he scrawled the opening line and a few other phrases of "Be Still, My Soul" on a scrap of paper. At his funeral they closed with this hymn, and the congregation stayed in their seats and sang it very quietly, in honor of the man who so lived out its lyrics.[1]

ICEBREAKER

Sometimes God rescues us on earth, as He did with the heroes listed in the first part of Hebrews 11. Other times His rescue is not on earth, as with the heroes at the close of Hebrews 11—they were sawn in two, stoned, and persecuted—but God gave them a "better resurrection."

Can you think of a time when God's rescue was not what you hoped, but was a real rescue? How was it a rescue, despite your suffering?

DAY 1: LETTING GO OF THE LIE

Before Beginning Your Private Study, Sing:

Using the CD, sing "Be Still, My Soul" along with Amy in your private quiet time.

Study:

Before we can speak the truth to our souls, we must expose a common lie that has permeated the body of Christ. This lie isn't coming only from flashy televangelists asking for your money and promising health and wealth in return; it also has slipped into popular Christian books and movies and been spread through the mouths of many well-meaning believers. What is the lie? It's an equation that looks like this:

Faith + good deeds = God's deliverance and blessing on earth

This is a lie that we *want* to believe, for it gives us control. We want to believe that if we have enough faith and live right, then God *has* to deliver us from plagues, poverty, and problems. Satan is clever—he knows better than to give us an outright lie, for we would spot it too easily. So he mixes the lie into the truth, hiding a little leaven in the flour, making it more palatable, and we swallow it. It is true that God is good and that He can and does heal on earth; that He does give many barren couples biological children; that He can and does deliver us from poverty and problems. But the lie, the leaven, is that that our faith and life can *guarantee* this.

Joni Eareckson Tada, who has lived most of her life in a wheelchair, says God's purpose is not to make us healthy, wealthy, or even happy (though it pleases Him to do so), but to make us holy. She continues: "Our pain, poverty, and broken hearts are not his ultimate focus. He cares about them, but ... God cares most—not about making us comfortable—but about teaching us to hate our sins, grow up spiritually, and love him."[2]

1. Read Hebrews 11:33–40.

   a. According to verses 33–35, how were some believers delivered on earth?

   b. How were some believers *not* delivered on earth? (vv. 35–38)

c. What does the author of Hebrews tell us about those who were not delivered? (vv. 39–40)

My husband was always pleased that he shared a name with one of the greatest saints of biblical history: Stephen. The book of Acts describes Stephen as "a man full of faith and of the Holy Spirit" (Acts 6:5). Yet religious leaders, concerned by the great wonders and miracles he was performing, seized him and produced false witnesses against him, saying "We have heard Stephen speak words of blasphemy against Moses and against God" (6:11). It makes sense to us, in our limited vision, that God would refute these lies and deliver Stephen, but instead Stephen is stoned to death. Let's consider the last hours of Stephen's life, beginning with the close of his magnificent sermon, which was filled with cutting and fearless truth.

2. Read Acts 7:51–60.

a. What facts in this part of Stephen's sermon (vv. 51–53) demonstrate historically that God doesn't always deliver the righteous on earth?

*b. How did the leaders respond? (v. 54) Why, do you think?

c. What truth does God give to Stephen that sustains him? (vv. 55–56)

*d. How do the leaders respond? (vv. 57–58) Why, do you think?

e. How did Stephen respond? How do you see Jesus in Stephen? (vv. 59−60)

Christianity spread like wildfire in the early days of the church, in part because of Christians' attitude when facing their own deaths. They were burned like torches, fed to the lions, and beheaded. In the second century, the author Tertullian observed: "The blood of the martyrs is the seed of the church."

Though it is true that God can and does deliver on earth, He sometimes has a deeper purpose. Sometimes we can see that purpose, and sometimes we must accept the mystery of suffering, knowing God is good. There are truths we can speak to our soul during these times, truths that will sustain us and conform us to the image of Christ.

3. Where have you heard the lie that if you believe and do what is right, you will be delivered from trouble on earth? How would you refute this? Why is it important that you do so?

DAY 2: GOD'S HEART

Before Beginning Your Private Study, Sing:

Memorize the first verse of "Be Still My Soul," filled with truth about God's heart for you. If you know Babbie Mason's song, "Trust His Heart," sing that as well.

Study:

4. Meditate on the title and repeated refrain, "Be Still, My Soul."

   ★a. Each word is monosyllabic. What do you remember about what monosyllabic words do?

b. How does the melody of "Finlandia" complement the words?

c. Meditate on the passage that inspired these words: Psalm 46:10. Of what are we to remind our souls?

> In the context of this passage, mountains are falling into the sea, waters are roaring and foaming (v. 2), yet God is still in control.

d. The New American Standard Bible (NASB) seems to come the closest to the Hebrew in its translation: "Cease striving and know that I am God." With that illumination, what would it mean for you to "be still" in your life right now?

Katherine von Schlegel wrote many rich verses for "Be Still, My Soul." The three that usually appear in hymnals, and the three that Amy sings, repeat the three reassurances found in the Psalter and all of Scripture, reminding us of God's:

- Heart
- History
- Heaven

5. What truths about God's heart for you stand out from the first verse of "Be Still My Soul"?

The only way I can "cease striving" when I don't understand what God is doing is to fall back on the fact that His heart is for me. I've always loved Babbie Mason's song that talks about how when we can't trace God's hand, we must trust His heart. New York City pastor Tim Keller was given seven minutes to speak at Ground Zero in Manhattan to families who had lost loved ones in that terrible, fiery 2001 tragedy. He told them that we cannot understand the reason God had for allowing 9/11, but we can know what the reason is *not.* It is *not* that God doesn't care. We'll look at a few scriptural evidences of God's heart that Keller gave. (You can hear this sermon online.[3])

6. Read Daniel 3.

a. What did Nebuchadnezzar make, and what order did he give? (vv. 1, 5)

b. What consequence was to come to those who disobeyed? (v. 6)

c. What did Shadrach, Meshach, and Abednego tell the king? (v. 16)

d. What did they know God could do? (v. 17)

e. What did they decide to do even if God did not rescue them? (v. 18)

f. How hot was the fire? (v. 22)

g. What miracles are described in verses 24–25? How does Nebuchadnezzar describe the fourth man?

Jesus was in the fire with Shadrach, Meshach, and Abednego. But it isn't until we get to the cross that we see how far He was willing to go to be in the fire with us.

7. Read Mark 14:32–43.

a. Apparently Jesus was given a foretaste of what His crucifixion would be like, for when He began to pray, something happened to Him. Describe it and His request as found in verses 33–34.

b. What did Jesus call God, and what did He ask of Him? (vv. 34–35)

c. What was His resolve if God did not let this cup pass from Him? (v. 36b)

d. What happened three times with His friends? (vv. 37–41)

★e. Did the above affect Jesus' resolve to go to the cross? Do you detect any faltering in verses 41–42? What do you see?

8. Read Isaiah 43:1–3.

   a. How does the Lord describe His relationship to us in verse 1?

   b. What promise does He make in verse 2?

   c. Why can we believe Him?

9. How do you see God's heart for you in each of the following lyrics? What exhortation, therefore, follows? Write down anything you see (or hear), reflecting on word pictures, melody, or other insights.

> Be still, my soul: the Lord is on thy side.
> Bear patiently the cross of grief or pain.
> Leave to thy God to order and provide;
> In every change, He faithful will remain.
> Be still, my soul: thy best, thy heav'nly Friend
> Through thorny ways leads to a joyful end.

DAY 3: GOD'S HISTORY

Before Beginning Your Private Study, Sing:

Memorize the second verse of "Be Still My Soul."

Study:

The second thread in this sturdy rope is to consider how God has been faithful to us in the past. When we simply cannot make sense of what God is doing now, it helps to look at what He has done before. That strengthens us to trust His character, wisdom, and timing.

Asaph was the psalmist who talked about "songs in the night."[4] Asaph's name means "collector," and he collected accounts of God's mercies to Israel. How did he do that? I suspect it might have been through memorized songs. Often miracles inspired songs, as when Miriam took up her tambourine after the parting of the Red Sea, and Deborah sang after defeating the Canaanite king. Asaph fathered "the sons of Asaph" who sang as they rebuilt the temple, rejoicing at what God was doing,[5] etching His mercies and miracles in their hearts. (My grandchildren go to a Christian classical school where they sing and sing and sing to remember the promises of Scripture, the miracles of God, the books of the Bible, the history of Christianity, and much more.) So when Asaph was despondent, when he asked the question of his soul, "Has God forgotten to be merciful?"[6] he knew the answer was a resounding no! Songs came to him in the night that helped him recount God's mercies.

10. Read Psalm 77.

  *a. As an overview, what characteristics of a classic lament can be seen in this psalm?

  b. Describe Asaph's emotions in verses 1–4.

  c. What does he choose to do, according to verses 5–6?

d. What value do you see of having songs about God's character and deeds committed to memory? (v. 6)

e. As Asaph's spirit mused, what questions does he ask in verses 7–9? As you state each question, find how a possibility of an answer comes in the second part of each verse:

v. 7 (Question and possibility of answer)

v. 8 (Question and possibility of answer)

v. 9 (Question and possibility of answer)

"This [passage] is a clear example of confessing one's doubts to the Lord. As the broad misgivings of verse 7 are spelled out more precisely in verse 8, their inner contradictions come to light, and with them, the possibility of an answer. If *steadfast love* is promised in His covenant, it can hardly disappear, or His promises come to nothing. The words *for ever* and *for all time* underline the point. And to ask 'Has God forgotten?' is to invite only one reply. The remaining question (9b) is admittedly more uncomfortable, since only sin arouses God's *anger*, and only impenitence perpetuates it. But that, if it arises, is a challenge rather than a problem."

DEREK KIDNER[7]

f. How does Asaph progress in turning away from his feelings to the Lord's character? (vv. 10–12)

g. What specific historical account does he remember in verses 13–20?

11. Psalm 78 is a continuation of Asaph remembering God's mighty deeds to His people in the past. A key verse is Psalm 78:11. What does it say?

12. In "Come Thou Fount" we learned about "raising our Ebenezer," finding physical ways to remember God's help to us in the past. Can you remember any way God helped you in your personal history in the following instances? If so, "raise your Ebenezer" by writing a specific and concise memory:

a. How did He help you at salvation, when you first received His forgiveness?

b. How did He help you in a time of great distress?

c. List one specific way He has enlarged your soul through suffering, truth, or mercy in the last few months.

13. Reflect on the following lyrics. Comment on how we are exhorted to remember God's historical goodness. Write down anything you see (or hear) as you meditate:

a. *Be still, my soul: thy God doth undertake to guide the future, as He has the past.*

⋆b. *Thy hope, thy confidence let nothing shake; all now mysterious shall be bright at last.*

c. *Be still, my soul: the waves and wind still know His voice who ruled them while He dwelt below.*

DAY 4: GOD'S HEAVEN

Before Beginning Your Private Study, Sing:

Sing the first two verses of "Be Still, My Soul" by heart, and the third verse looking at the words.

Study:

Most of us have not had to endure life-threatening persecution, hunger, or slavery. But believers who have endured such traumas were sustained by their hope of a very different life one day. African-American spirituals have a common theme: heaven. In heaven they knew they would lay down their burdens, see justice roll down like a river, and be reunited with the spouses and children from whom they were cruelly separated.

After Steve died, the children and I had such a longing to know more about heaven. Because heaven is so mysterious and because the prophets speak in symbols of golden streets and pearly gates, I also felt fear, and confessed those to the Lord in my prayer journal:

Friday, October 22
Two days after burying Steve

Everyone has left except the girls and me. O Lord—what is it like for Steve? Will I really see him, touch him, talk to him again?

Heaven scares me. I'm afraid it will be so ethereal. I don't really like the thought of gold streets, or enormous mansions, or no marriage. It all sounds a little cold. I want Steve to be happy.

Help us understand, Lord.

My growing understanding of poetry in Scripture has indeed helped me not to take the gold streets and pearly gates verbatim, but as similes representing the very best. We also received many copies of two books, both titled *Heaven*, by two separate authors: Randy Alcorn and Joni Eareckson Tada. Both wrote convincingly of a very different heaven than many of us imagine. Both had fears, like mine, that God put to rest. The most encouraging and revolutionary scriptural truth that both shared is that heaven is not someplace far away where angels play harps on clouds, but it is very tangible, very real—and very much like earth except that all the ravages of sin will be removed. Scripture tells us that God continually makes things new, and that is what He is going to do with the earth. Instead of wiping out the earth, heaven is going to come down and earth will be transformed. The best will remain, but there will be no more weeds, no more earthquakes, no more hurricanes, no more pollution, and no more death.

We also will see our loved ones who are in the Lord. Just as Jesus had a real body that could move, live, and breathe—so will our loved ones. Again—they will not be ethereal but tangible.

Just as Jesus could eat, laugh, and speak—so will we. What will vanish are sickness, sorrow, and sin.

My husband's rich voice, which was made raspy through cancer, will be restored, and we will talk, and laugh, and enjoy a heaven and earth more beautiful than the first snow falling on fir trees, or the most glorious summer sunset over the ocean. I think about how in heaven the arm that our daughter Beth lost as a baby will be restored. (She'll be able to bike and to swim easily with us!) John and Julie will meet the babies they miscarried. My mother, who endured the pain of childhood sexual abuse and suffered her whole life from it, will be completely healed. And just think—our sin nature will be gone! Hosea prophesies that there is coming a day when God "will remove the names of the Baals"[8] from our lips. Our sinful desires that reach toward false objects of worship will be removed! No more lust toward ambition, sexual immorality, or gluttony. No more clinging too tightly to a good thing. Instead, that insatiable black hole in our souls will be filled beyond our wildest imaginations with the joy and peace that come from Jesus. And everything good, like friendship and food, will remain without distortion, or, like sex and marriage, be replaced with something even better.

14. Read John 14:1–3.

    a. What three commands does Jesus give in verse 1?

    b. What do you learn about heaven in verse 2? What reassurance is tucked in between the facts?

    c. What promise is given in verse 3?

d. How do these lyrics reflect the above truths?

> Be still, my soul: the hour is hastening on
> When we shall be forever with the Lord.

15. Read Isaiah's prophecy of heaven in Isaiah 25:6–9.

⋆a. How does verse 6 make it clear that heaven will be tangible rather than ethereal?

⋆b. What shroud will God destroy, according to verses 7–8? (Remember parallelism, and see how verse 8a helps to explain 7.)

⋆c. What three promises do you find in verse 8?

⋆d. How do the following lyrics reflect the above truths?

> When disappointment, grief, and fear are gone,
> Sorrow forgot, love's purest joys restored.

16. Read Revelation 21:1–5.

   ★a. Rather than our going "up" into heaven, as many people believe, what is actually going to happen, according to verses 1–2?

   ★b. Who is the bride who is coming down out of heaven? (see also Revelation 19:7–8 and 5:9–10)

   c. What promises are given in Revelation 21:3–4?

   ★d. What does Jesus tell us in verse 5? How does this fit with God's pattern of renewal and reformation rather than destruction?

   e. What comfort do you find in knowing that the best of earth will not be destroyed but renewed? What comfort do you find in the tangible aspects of heaven?

f. How do the following lyrics reflect the above truths?

> Be still, my soul: when change and tears are past,
> All safe and blessed we shall meet at last.

DAY 5: THEN SHALT THOU BETTER KNOW HIS HEART

Before Beginning Your Private Study, Sing:

Sing by heart as much as you can of "Be Still, My Soul."

Study:

On the third anniversary of Steve's death I was at our Wisconsin cabin, where I always hope to be on that day, where I can go to Steve's grave. It was a day of such sad memories, but I woke to find this dear email from my youngest daughter, Annie.

Hi Mom

I found some more lyrics to "Be Still, My Soul"—I don't know if you've seen them or not. I'm learning the chords so we can sing it together. It is a good song. I hope it comforts you today.

> Be still, my soul: when dearest friends depart,
> And all is darkened in the vale of tears,
> Then shalt thou better know His love, His heart,
> Who comes to soothe thy sorrow and thy fears.
> Be still, my soul: thy Jesus can repay
> From His own fullness all He takes away.

I wish I could hang out with you. Sometimes a girl just wants her mom!

Annie

I thanked God for my daughter's love and for this powerful verse. I sang, sang, sang it that day.

I do better know His love, His heart than I did five years ago. Suffering either drives us away from God or into His arms. If it drives us into His arms, we do better know His love, His heart.

17. Meditate on the additional verse to "Be Still, My Soul" from the letter on page 119. What stands out to you? Why?

18. If you read chapter 6 of the book *The God of All Comfort,* what stood out to you and why?

19. What will you remember from this week's lesson? Why?

Group Prayer Time

Circle in a small group. Begin with prayers of thanksgiving for ways God has shown His heart to you, has been faithful to you in the past, or has given you hope through heaven. Then lift up areas of need and allow the others to support you. Close by singing the first verse of "Be Still, My Soul."

A Mighty Fortress*

A mighty fortress is our God, a Bulwark never failing;
Our Helper He, amid the flood of mortal ills prevailing:
For still our ancient foe doth seek to work us woe;
His craft and pow'r are great, and, armed with cruel hate,
On earth is not his equal.

Did we in our own strength confide, our striving would be losing;
Were not the right Man on our side, the Man of God's own choosing:
Dost ask who that may be? Christ Jesus, it is He;
Lord Sabbaoth, His name, from age to age the same,
And He must win the battle.

And though this world, with devils filled, should threaten to undo us,
We will not fear, for God hath willed His truth to triumph through us.
The Prince of Darkness grim, we tremble not for him;
His rage we can endure, for lo, his doom is sure,
One little word shall fell him.

That Word above all earthly pow'rs, no thanks to them, abideth;
The Spirit and the gifts are ours through Him who with us sideth.
Let goods and kindred go, this mortal life also;
The body they may kill: God's truth abideth still,
His kingdom is forever.

Words and Music by: Martin Luther, 1529
Translated from German to English by: Frederic H. Hedge, 1853
Arr. by: Amy S. Wixtrom and Gary Wixtrom, 2009
©2009 G. B. WIX Publishing ASCAP

*Available on the companion music CD

THOUGH THE MOUNTAINS FALL INTO THE SEA

(Hymn: "A Mighty Fortress")

SHORTLY AFTER STEVE'S DIAGNOSIS, SALLY TOLD HER DAD SHE WANTED TO SING A SOLO FOR HIM in church that following Sunday. "What would you like me to sing?"

"A Mighty Fortress," Steve said with conviction.

"A Mighty Fortress," inspired by Psalm 46, and written by Martin Luther, is a song for a battle. It was Luther's theme song during the Reformation, as he fought the corruption that had polluted the gospel. Some church leaders were even selling indulgences to family members who wanted to rescue a loved one from hell. Luther knew the battle wasn't so much against the authorities of the present church, but against unseen forces who were suppressing the truth that we are saved by faith alone. During this time, when he needed courage for the battle, Luther would often say to his friend Philip Melanchthon, "Come, Philip, let us sing the forty-sixth."[1]

"A Mighty Fortress" became our theme song during our personal battle. I'll never forget what happened when she sang.

Sunday, August 17
Two weeks after Steve's diagnosis

Sally sang "A Mighty Fortress" in church this morning. Annie and Beth on one side of Steve, pressed into him, me on the other. John in the pew behind with his hand on Steve's shoulder. Sally sang it as a fighting song—I'd never heard it sung that way—I don't think I'd ever really understood it before. I've heard it sung majestically, but never with righteous anger. Yet, it seemed so right. It is a call to battle against Satan and all the spiritual workers of darkness. Sally kept shaking her fist at Satan, at "the prince of darkness grim," at the one "armed with cruel hate," at the one who must not "this battle win." Each verse grew stronger, and our hearts found courage for the fight ahead. But when Sally got to the phrase, "let goods and kindred go, this mortal life also," she looked at Steve and faltered. It was too much for her, and she stopped, paralyzed with grief. Suddenly—and I will never in all my life forget this—Judy *[the pianist]* began to sing, then the congregation rose—standing in the gap for us, finishing Sally's song for her. They are with us.

Truly, as "A Mighty Fortress" expresses, we were in a battle with the enemy. In the beginning we thought that the enemy was cancer. But there was a much more deadly battle going on—a battle for our lives to glorify God. If Steve or his family would despair of God, then Satan would have succeeded in destroying our testimony. He longed to do that, and his fiercest way of attacking us was to tell us lies about God. Satan's lie, which Luther exposed during the Reformation, was "You have to earn God's love." The lie Satan whispers in suffering is, "You have lost God's love."

ICEBREAKER

Was there ever a time when you thought you had to earn God's love? When you thought the way to go to heaven was to do good things? If so, how did the truth break through? (Share in one sentence, one breath.)

DAY 1: FOR STILL OUR ANCIENT FOE

Before Beginning Your Private Study, Sing:

Imagine that you are in the midst of a battle for your soul. Imagine that tomorrow you are going to be asked to choose between denying Christ publicly or dying a martyr's death. Or imagine that you are dying of cancer and feel tempted to blaspheme God. You don't want to deny Christ, but you are afraid you might. Sing "A Mighty Fortress" along with Amy on the CD to prepare yourself. Shake your fist at the enemy. Sing all four verses with conviction—thinking about how it is a song designed to give you courage for the battle. Sing with anger against the enemy; sing with escalation into victory! Sing!

Study:

"A Mighty Fortress" is a hymn that has to have all four verses sung, for it is a problem that builds to a victory. Our problem is that we have an ancient foe who wants us to despair of God. He wants to create "attachment disorder" between us and our heavenly Father.

Steve and I adopted our two youngest children from overseas orphanages. Beth was twelve years old when we brought her into our home, and she had never known human love. Through what we believe was some kind of abuse, she lost her arm as an infant. Her birth parents abandoned her on the street, leaving her to die. In the orphanage she also experienced abuse. When she came to us, as is common with children with her kind of history, she had trouble trusting, trouble "attaching" to people, even people who loved her. She'd flinch when we'd touch her, laugh nervously when we'd affirm her, and retreat frequently to her room. (In time, through the persistent love of her family and the body of Christ, and through God showing her His love in so many ways, we have seen great healing.) Attachment disorder is common among children who have been abused by those who should have protected them.

"Attachment disorder" is what Satan longs to see happen in us as children of God. He whispers to us the lie that the One who should have protected us has abandoned us. His method, beginning in the garden, is to cast doubt on God's goodness and love for His children. And when suffering comes into our lives, that hungry lion smells blood and comes out of his den, seeking a vulnerable object of prey, circling us without mercy. He snarls and whispers that we have failed God and therefore we have lost God's love. The One who should have protected us has withdrawn, and so we should withdraw from Him.

Our real battle is not against the temporary but difficult circumstances of this world, and not against flesh and blood, but against our enemy who wants us to despair of God and let go of our only true lifeline. We are in a battle with the Prince of this Earth for our very souls. We must win the battle!

Sing the first verse of "A Mighty Fortress" again, noting the absolute declarative phrases, the "o" sounds, the firm monosyllables, the seriousness and strength of the music.

> A mighty fortress is our God, a Bulwark never failing;
> Our Helper He, amid the flood of mortal ills prevailing:
> For still our ancient foe doth seek to work us woe;
> His craft and pow'r are great, and, armed with cruel hate,
> On earth is not his equal.

1. Reflect on what the first verse of this hymn teaches about our God.

   a. What word picture is used to describe God in the first two lines? If you were an artist, how might you draw this?

   ★b. Read the first word picture in Psalm 46:1–3 that inspired Luther's lyrics. Something that is often regarded as strong and trustworthy fails. What is it? (vv. 2–3) What is the contrast? (v. 1)

★c. Think of a blessing, other than God, that you might build your life around (a person, career, etc.) but which could be shaken, like a mountain falling into the sea.

2. Let's next turn our focus to our enemy, Satan.

★a. After each of the following descriptions of Satan, write down your reflections. Because this is poetry, the language is intense, that is, there is much in it, like a rich chocolate cake. Take your time; don't gobble it down. Think about the meaning of the words; sing aloud the sounds of the vowels, the rhyme, the meter. Note anything you discover through your senses, all the time asking God to help you.

- *Ancient foe*

- *Doth seek to work us woe*

- *His craft and pow'r are great*

- *And armed with cruel hate*

- *On earth is not his equal*

b. Now look up the related passages and write down how they illustrate each of these phrases:

- *Ancient foe* (Job 1:6–7)

- *Doth seek to work us woe* (1 Peter 5:8)

- *His craft and pow'r are great* (Genesis 3:1; John 8:44)

- *And armed with cruel hate* (Job 2:4–5)

- *On earth is not his equal* (John 12:31; 14:30; 16:11)

★3. Think about a spiritual battle you have been in, or perhaps are in right now. What lie would the enemy like you to believe? Why?

DAY 2: DID WE IN OUR OWN STRENGTH CONFIDE

Before Beginning Your Private Study, Sing:

Memorize the first verse of "A Mighty Fortress," singing it until you need no notes. Then sing the second verse, thinking about every phrase as you sing.

Study:

August 31

Six weeks before Steve's death

My dear sister Sally is organizing a forty-day fast for Steve. Believers throughout the world are planning to do various kinds of fasts, praying for my husband, that he might win the battle.

Today Steve told Sally that he was thinking of the battle a bit differently than we are. He sees this as a fight to glorify God in his suffering. He was reflecting on a story from one of Pastor Mike's sermons, in which one persecuted believer was so confident he would never deny the Lord that he didn't ask for prayer. Another was fearful he would give up and deny God, so pleaded with friends to pray that he would not "confide in his own strength." The first denied the Lord in the midst of his suffering, but the other glorified God, even as he was being burned at the stake.

I said to Steve, "You would never deny the Lord." Steve reminded me that that is what Peter thought, but Peter did deny the Lord. Jesus had warned Peter that Satan was going to sift him. Steve feels he is being "sifted."

O God—the same foe that stalked Job and Peter is stalking and sifting my precious husband. Our enemy is "armed with cruel hate."

Please, God, fight for Steve. Sustain him in the midst of his intense suffering. He longs to glorify you to the end.

May it not be the end. But if it is, help him, O God.

Sing the second verse of "A Mighty Fortress" again. Sing reflectively; sing for the battles you will face today.

> Did we in our own strength confide, our striving would be losing;
> Were not the right Man on our side, the Man of God's own choosing:
> Dost ask who that may be? Christ Jesus, it is He;
> Lord Sabbaoth, His name, from age to age the same,
> And He must win the battle.

4. *Did we in our own strength confide, our striving would be losing*

    a. Put the warning of the second verse's opening line in your own words.

    b. What does 1 Corinthians 10:12 say?

    c. Using your imagination, what pictures does the word *striving* bring to mind?

All other religions tell you to strive and to work for your salvation and for victory in life's battles. Only Christianity tells you to rest in Christ for your salvation and for victory in life's battles. When Buddha died he exhorted, "Keep striving." When Christ died, He said, "It is finished."

    d. In context, Luther's word *striving* is similar to the word Jesus uses for *spin* or *toil* when talking about the lilies in Matthew 6:28. What is the picture here and what application can we make?

5. *Were not the right Man on our side; the Man of God's own choosing*

    a. Satan wants us to believe God is not for us. What does this line of "A Mighty Fortress" tell us?

    b. Often during suffering, Satan whispers that God is not for us. How does Romans 8:31–32 refute that? What proof is given?

★6. Find the question in the third line of this verse. What is it? How does this help portray Luther's irritation?

7. *Lord Sabbaoth His name, from age to age the same*

    a. Sabbaoth is derived from the Latin word *sabaoth*, and means "army" or "hosts." In other words, Jesus is Lord of all the hosts—the good angels and the bad angels. What does this tell you about His power over Satan?

    b. What does 1 John 4:4 tell us?

c. Satan can't do anything without permission from God. How do you see this in Job 1:12?

⋆d. From age to age, God has only given Satan enough rope to hang himself. What was Satan's wager in Job 1:11? How did Satan lose that battle?

8. What battles might you be facing today? How can they be won, according to what you learned today?

DAY 3: HIS RAGE WE CAN ENDURE, FOR LO, HIS DOOM IS SURE

Before Beginning Your Private Study, Sing:

Memorize the second verse of "A Mighty Fortress," singing it until you need no notes. Sing both the first and second verse without notes, thinking about every phrase as you sing.

Study:

Because Satan is the prince of this world, and because his main purpose is to get us to despair of God, we should not be surprised when life is hard.

I wanted, with all my heart, to not have Steve suffer. But he did. I wanted so to protect my children from suffering. I asked God not to take our children's father. But they lost their father for their remaining time on earth. Satan rages. But he cannot be victorious.

My husband won the real battle, the battle for his soul. He glorified God to the end. My children, though they have suffered, have also grown. Their souls have been enlarged. They are not the same people they were before this happened. God only gave the enemy enough rope to hang himself.

February 1
Four years, four months since Steve's death

I'm visiting Sally in snowy Chicago. We went to see the play, Screwtape Letters *[based on the book by C. S. Lewis describing the strategies of "Screwtape," Lewis's name for Satan]*, and it certainly made us think about this battle we are in with our ancient foe.

The play takes place in Screwtape's dark den in hell. Screwtape himself is played by Max McLean, but there is also a small woman gymnast who plays a catlike demon: hissing, scratching, and cavorting about the stage. She lithely climbs a ladder to a chute that sends and receives the correspondence from Screwtape to his apprentice on earth, Wormwood. When the letter brings the good news that they have been successful in deceiving the client, causing him to despair of God's love, this demon leaps gleefully from the ladder and rolls on the floor with a hyena-like laugh. But when the news is bad, when the client is actually trusting God despite his suffering, she claws the air and screeches.

As we drove home, I asked Sally how she was different than she was five years ago, after all we've experienced. She said, "I know there is a purpose in suffering. So no matter what, I win. If God gives me the desire of my heart, then that is a great blessing. But if He does not, if He allows me to suffer loss, then there is a purpose. My character is made stronger, and one day, the lower I am taken on earth, the higher I will soar in heaven. I know this." Then she clawed the air in a catlike gesture and screeched.

We both laughed.

Sing the third verse of "A Mighty Fortress" as a battle song, thinking about the phrases as you sing.

> And though this world, with devils filled, should threaten to undo us,
> We will not fear, for God hath willed, His truth to triumph through us.
> The Prince of Darkness grim, we tremble not for him;
> His rage we can endure, for lo, his doom is sure,
> One little word shall fell him.

9. What does the first line of the third stanza tell us?

10. What does Ephesians 6:12 teach?

★11. This third verse contains some clever rhymes that are also contrasts between Satan and God. See if you can find them. What same truth do they all teach?

12. Read the poem in Revelation 12:10–12.

    a. What will happen to the one who accuses us day and night? (v. 10)

    b. How were believers able to overcome Satan? (v. 11)

    c. Why is the devil filled with rage or fury? (v. 12)

13. If "the mountains are falling into the sea" in your life, if you are in the midst of Satan's rage, what truth can sustain you?

DAY 4: ONE LITTLE WORD WILL FELL HIM

Before Beginning Your Private Study, Sing:

Memorize the third verse of "A Mighty Fortress," singing it until you need no notes. Sing the first three verses of the song, thinking about every phrase as you sing. (If this overwhelms you, then do what you can.)

Study:

Life is hard and getting harder. Recently I heard Sara Groves share in concert how she came to write "A Song for My Sons" in which she repeatedly warns them not to let their love grow cold. Her lyrics were inspired by Matthew 24—the chapter in which Jesus describes the increasing hardship and persecution that will occur at the end of the age, and which includes this phrase: "the love of most will grow cold" (v. 12).

These are the truths we need to breathe to our soul as life gets harder and persecution increases:

> That Word above all earthly pow'rs, no thanks to them, abideth;
> The Spirit and the gifts are ours through Him who with us sideth.
> Let goods and kindred go, this mortal life also;
> The body they may kill: God's truth abideth still,
> His kingdom is forever.

★14. Let's take a closer look at these phrases in the fourth verse of "A Might Fortress" as we learn what we can do so that our love doesn't grow cold.

a. *That Word above all earthly pow'rs, no thanks to them, abideth*

Put this idea in your own words. If you don't understand it, 1 John 2:15–17 might help you.

b. *The Spirit and the gifts are ours*

What contrast do you see between these "possessions" and the things of this world?

   c. *Let goods and kindred go, this mortal life also*

This was the phrase that our daughter had trouble singing when she looked at her dad in church the Sunday after his diagnosis. But when she sang this same hymn at his funeral, she was able to sing it with power. Why can we let our loved ones and our own lives go if we know the Lord? (see 1 Thessalonians 4:13–18)

   d. *The body they may kill: God's truth abideth still, His kingdom is forever*

How might this truth help you to stay strong should you have to face martyrdom for your faith?

15. What observations can you make concerning the melody, meter, and strength of this final verse of "A Mighty Fortress"?

DAY 5: YOU CAN NEITHER EARN NOR LOSE GOD'S LOVE

Before Beginning Your Private Study, Sing:

Memorize the fourth verse of "A Mighty Fortress," singing it until you need no notes.

   Sing as much as you can of "A Mighty Fortress." Sing for your battles now, and for the battles you will face. Sing, sing, sing.

Study:

You Cannot Earn God's Love

"A Mighty Fortress" became the theme song of the Reformation. The church had become corrupted in doctrine and practice, teaching that we earn our salvation. Luther's battle was against this greatest of lies, and he ignited a storm when he nailed a document describing the corruption on the door of the Castle Church in Wittenberg, Germany, in 1517. The storm brewed and built until, in 1521, Emperor Charles V summoned Luther to appear before civil and ecclesiastical authorities in the city of Worms to be offered one more opportunity to recant.

Luther was afraid, as the stoutest of believers would have been. It was a struggle between the fear of man and the fear of God. He needed strength for the battle and he found it in the Word, and in all the scriptural truths he expressed in "A Mighty Fortress." The movie *Luther* (MGM, 2003) accurately shows his fear, but then, his courage when he made his famous statement to the Imperial Court.

> Unless I am convinced by Scripture or evident reason (for I trust neither in popes nor in councils alone, since it is obvious that they have often erred and contradicted themselves) I am convicted by the Scripture which I have mentioned and my conscience is captive to the Word of God. Therefore I cannot and will not recant, since it is difficult, unprofitable and dangerous, indeed to do anything against one's conscience. God help me. Amen.[2]

The Reformation was a mighty victory, but the battle continues. Satan continues to lie, to corrupt, and to confuse.

You Cannot Lose God's Love

A corollary to the lie that we must earn God's love is that we can lose God's love. For if we earned it, then, indeed, we can lose it. If you are a Christian, but the gospel has not truly transformed your heart and mind, you are apt to believe one of these corollary lies of the enemy:

Lie #1: Because God's love is contingent on how good a person you are, you must be breaking the rules, or this suffering would not be coming into your life. This is what Job's friends told him. Let's battle this lie with the truth.

16. What did God tell Job's friends in Job 42:7–9?

17. On what is God's love contingent according to Titus 3:3–7?

18. If you believe the lie that you can lose God's love, then when suffering comes into your life, you hate yourself. Peter had these feelings after he denied the Lord three times. How does God make sure Peter knows he is still loved after his failure? (Mark 16:7)

19. Read Luke 15:11–24.

   a. How did the younger son fail the father? (vv. 11–13)

   b. How did he come to his senses? (vv. 14–19)

   c. How do you think this son expected the father to respond?

   d. How did the father respond? (vv. 20–24)

Lie #2: This lie goes like this: Because God's love is contingent on how good a person you are, and because you have tried very hard, God is being unfair. You cannot trust Him.

The parable you began to study in the last question is often truncated, with people thinking Jesus' main point was about God's love for the sinner (the younger son). That is *a* true point, but the main point actually follows. Jesus told this story to the Pharisees (see Luke 15:1–2), who believed they could earn God's love by right living. Jesus' central point is not about the "prodigal" son, but the contrast between him and the older brother.

20. Read Luke 15:25–32.

  a. Describe the older brother's attitude in verses 25–28.

  b. Why does he feel he has earned the right to his father's love and blessings? (v. 29)

  c. Why does he feel that his father is being unfair?

  ⋆d. What does the older son fail to understand?

21. When suffering comes into your life, how will you refute these two lies of the enemy?

  a. Lie #1: You have lost God's love by not keeping the rules.

  b. Lie #2: God is being unfair because you have tried hard to keep the rules.

> "Preach the gospel to yourself every day."
> JERRY BRIDGES

> The Lord Almighty is with us;
> The God of Jacob is our fortress.
>
> PSALM 46:7, 11

22. If you read chapter 7 of the book *The God of All Comfort,* what stood out to you?

23. What do you think you will remember about this week's lesson? Why?

GROUP PRAYER TIME

Circle in groups of three and four for conversational prayer. Using question 23 as a springboard, share your answer and allow the others to pray that God will seal it in your heart, helping you to remember it.

Abide with Me, My Redeemer*

Abide with me, fast falls the eventide;
The darkness deepens, Lord with me abide.
When other helpers fail and comforts flee,
Help of the helpless, Lord abide.

I fear no foe, with Thee at hand to bless;
Ills have no weight, and tears no bitterness;
Where is death's sting? Where grave, thy victory?
I triumph still, if Thou abide.

I know that my Redeemer lives
Hold Thou Thy cross before my closing eyes;
Shine through the gloom, and point me to the skies.
Heav'n's morning breaks, and earth's vain shadows flee;
In life, in death, O Lord abide.

I know that my Redeemer lives,
And I will see Him with my eyes.

Yet in death, I will see Him
in my flesh, I will see God.

Abide with me,
Abide with me.

Words by: Henry F. Lyte, 1847 (and from the book of Job)
Music by: "Abide," William H. Monk, 1861 "Redeemer,"
     George Frederic Handel, 1741
Additional music written by: Amy Shreve Wixtrom
     and Gary Wixtrom, 2009
Arr. by: Amy S. Wixtrom and Gary Wixtrom, 2009
©2009 G. B. Wix Publishing ASCAP

* Available on the companion music CD

I KNOW
MY REDEEMER LIVES

(Medley: "Abide with Me, My Redeemer")

AMY SHREVE WIXTROM AND GARY WIXTROM HAVE BEAUTIFULLY BLENDED THE CLASSIC, "ABIDE with Me," and Handel's "I Know That My Redeemer Liveth." Both of these masterpieces share the theme of hope when facing death. "Abide with Me" is a reflective lament, filled with soft "s" sounds. "I Know That My Redeemer Liveth," which becomes the chorus in this medley, is the stronger foundation, the hope that is the answer.

ICEBREAKER

Have you ever sung or attended a performance of Handel's *Messiah*? If so, share a reflection on any of the pieces from it, or a memory from the experience.

Or,

Have you ever been present when a believer has died? Share a memory.

DAY 1: THE DARKNESS DEEPENS

Before Beginning Your Private Study, Sing:

Listen to Amy's "Abide with Me, My Redeemer," singing as you can. Then memorize the first verse. You may also want to listen to the classic hymn on iTunes or the Cyberhymnal online.

Study:

If nothing else convinces us we are not in control, death certainly does. When we received Steve's diagnosis, few words could comfort me. I had an invisible knife sticking out of my heart, and those who pressed up against me with pat answers or even Scripture pressed that knife to excruciating depths of pain. What I needed was people to "sit shiva" with me, to weep with me. When I called to tell my sister Bonnie the news, that is exactly what she did.

Sunday, August 10
Right after Steve's diagnosis

Yesterday I called Bonnie *[my sister]* to tell her. She cried. Was shocked. Then she cried more. She tried to talk, but she couldn't.

A few hours later she called back to tell me she was sorry that she had been so out of control. I told her that her tears had ministered to me more than anything. Then she tried to pray for me by singing "Abide with Me." She cried again as she sang—so much that if I didn't know it already I wouldn't have understood a word. I'll always remember her sobbing song:

> Abide with me! Fast falls the eventide.
> The darkness deepens; Lord with me abide!
> When other helpers fail and comforts flee,
> Help of the helpless, oh, abide with me!

No answers. No judgments. Just a cry to the Help of the Helpless to abide with me.

Henry Lyte, a nineteenth-century Anglican pastor, wrote the lyrics of "Abide with Me" just three weeks before his death, his health rapidly deteriorating.

1. Meditate on the first verse of "Abide with Me."

   ⋆a. What qualities of a lament do you see in it?

b. How does the music correspond to the lyrics of this lament?

c. What word pictures stand out to you? Why?

Henry Lyte said that "Abide with Me" was inspired by his meditation on the walk to Emmaus in Luke 24.

2. Read the first part of this story in Luke 24:13–24.

a. Describe the mood of the two disciples. (v. 17) What does this tell you concerning their confidence in the women's story that Christ was alive?

★b. What humor do you see in this encounter?

3. Read the second part of the story in Luke 24:25–35.

a. Where did Jesus begin in the Scriptures to show Himself to these men?

It is both faith-building and thrilling to know that Jesus can be seen from Genesis through Revelation. In fact, as Tim Keller so frequently says, "Every prophet, every priest, every bridegroom, every slain lamb, every suffering servant ... points to a better Prophet, a better Priest, a better Bridegroom."

b. Though they *still* didn't recognize Him, they longed for Him to stay. What did they ask of Him in verse 29, and what reason did they give?

c. How can you see the above words in the first verse of "Abide with Me"? How does Lyte use the idea of the fast-approaching night as a metaphor for death?

Though his health was failing rapidly, just before Henry Lyte wrote this hymn he is said to have nearly crawled to the pulpit for one last sermon to encourage his congregation to "prepare for the solemn hour which must come to all."[1]

4. Are you prepared for the solemn hour of your death? If so, explain. If not, cry out to the only One who can help you.

DAY 2: WHEN OTHER HELPERS FAIL AND COMFORTS FLEE

Before Beginning Your Private Study, Sing:

Memorize the first verse of "Abide with Me" and sing it in your time alone with the Lord.

Study:

Job's friends certainly failed him in his greatest hour of need, actually increasing his suffering. They have become known as the "miserable comforters," a term Job used for them.

If you remember, at the very beginning of Job's troubles, his friends did something right. They "sat shiva" with him, keeping him silent company for seven days. Perhaps this empathy, this sitting shiva on the part of his three friends, is what gives Job the courage to at last release his lament. Before this he has said all the "right" things, all the "spiritual" things. But now it is as if his pain has been unlocked, and his honest thoughts come gushing out. The very first thing Job does after his friends sit shiva is to curse, not God, but the day of his birth:

> May the day of my birth perish,
>> and the night it was said, "A boy is born!"
>>> Job 3:3

His friends do not approve! Though Job is being honest with God, and though God does not condemn him for this, his friends certainly do. Now the empathetic silence is past and the pointing fingers, the pontificating sermons, and the pious condemnations begin—and persist relentlessly for thirty-four long chapters. Job's friends spoke true principles, but misapplied them to Job. They made mistakes that people commonly make about suffering. Though it is true that we reap what we sow, that was *not* the reason for Job's suffering. How can we possibly know why someone loses health, a loved one, or a ministry? Only God can see the heart, only God has the answer. (We know from the end of the story in Job 42 that Job's friends were wrong, for God told them so and asked them to repent and ask for Job's forgiveness.)

5. Eliphaz is the first "miserable comforter" whose fatherly attitude is betrayed by a cold, cold heart. His "counsel" can be summarized in his words of Job 4:8. What does he tell Job? What is the implication?

★6. What does Proverbs 22:8 say? How has Eliphaz misused this "proverb" about sowing and reaping when it comes to Job?

★7. What does Eliphaz tell Job in Job 4:6? How is this advice wrong? Where should our confidence be?

*8. Eliphaz tells Job of a dream in Job 4:12–17. Though Eliphaz seems to believe it is from God, there is abundant evidence it is from the evil one. (Remember, he is constantly on the prowl, wanting us to believe we have lost God's love.) What marks of the enemy can you find in the spirit and message of this dream?

9. What is Job's lament in Job 6:14?

10. What warnings can you find from Eliphaz about:

a. What we should say or not say when a friend is suffering?

b. How the enemy may use us to cause the suffering to despair of God?

*c. How dreams and visions need to be checked by the Word of God?

11. In what ways can you see Job as a shadow of the coming Suffering Servant? How did the friends of Jesus also let Him down in His greatest hour of need? (see Mark 14:32–42)

12. When other helpers fail and comforts flee, who is equipped to "sit shiva" with you? Why?

DAY 3: I KNOW THAT MY REDEEMER LIVETH

Before Beginning Your Private Study, Sing:

If possible, rent a CD of Handel's *Messiah* from your local library and listen to "I Know That My Redeemer Liveth," or buy it on iTunes. Or, watch a performance on the Internet (I like the one by Lynn Dawson). You may also choose to watch Nicole C. Mullen's contemporary version.

Sing "Abide with Me, My Redeemer" with Amy.

Study:

It is said that Frederic Handel composed the *Messiah* in twenty-four days, never leaving his home and often skipping meals. When he was writing the "Hallelujah Chorus," his servant reported that Handel exclaimed: "I did think I did see all of Heaven before me, and the great God Himself!"[2]

The passage from Job that provides the lyrics for "I Know That My Redeemer Liveth" was likewise the result of an ecstatic vision given to Job. It is famous not only for its inspiration, giving hope and heart to sufferers throughout time, but for its illumination—for it teaches us so much about heaven!

Though Job's miserable comforters were continually interrupting his lament to God, Job persists, and in the midst of his laments, God does come to him—three times. The following instance, perhaps because of Handel's *Messiah*, is the best known.

13. Read Job 19:13–22 and list some of his laments.

14. What request does Job make in Job 19:23–24?

15. Now, in response, comes the vision of the second coming of Christ that takes our breath away — especially when we consider that Job was written at least 1,500 years before the first time Christ came to earth. In the space below write out Job 19:25–27 as an aid in contemplation. (You may want to look at this passage in a few translations.)

16. Record your observations on these verses.

   a. What is the first statement? (v. 25a)

   b. What does the word *redeem* mean?

The actual Hebrew word here, *Go-el*, was "a delicious word, a passionate word, a word that smacked of chains falling off, of finding buried treasure."[3] God had a merciful law to protect widows who had no children. If she had a near relative, that man was her "Go-el" who had a responsibility to protect her, to rescue her, and to continue the family line. Boaz in the book of

Ruth is an illustration of this; he protected, provided, and passionately loved Ruth—rescuing her and Naomi from poverty and ensuring that their family line was not snuffed out.

    c. How has Christ paid the ransom for us, rescued us from poverty, and guaranteed us an inheritance that can never fade?

    d. Where, according to Job 19:25b, will we see Jesus?

"The Bible plainly teaches that the resurrection is not a phenomenon that will transpire up in Heaven but rather—much more shockingly—right here on earth. Here is where death occurs; here is where the dead will rise. To dust our bodies were consigned; from dust they will be reclaimed. Listen: the very graves will open their mouths, and the dead will spring out of them and begin walking around—just as Jesus did on Easter morning!"

MIKE MASON, *The Gospel According to Job*[4]

    e. How does Revelation 21:1–2 parallel Job 19:25?

God is not going to destroy the earth totally, but renew it. Heaven and earth will be joined. Heaven will be the best of earth, with all the effects of the fall forever taken away.

f. Will we be ghostlike in heaven? What does Job 19:26 say?

g. How has Job's misery been temporarily transformed? (v. 27)

h. How does this picture of heaven give you hope?

17. How has the plea in Job 19:23–24 been answered?

DAY 4: I Fear No Foe

Before Beginning Your Private Study, Sing:

Sing the second verse of "Abide with Me, My Redeemer" along with Amy. This verse from the classic hymn "Abide with Me" teaches truths that Job learned in his first ecstatic vision. This vision is not as famous as the one you just studied in Day 3, but it is absolutely fascinating.

Study:

Job did not have what we have, living on this side of the cross. The afterlife in the Old Testament was a shadowy world, and you often see God's people expressing fear and doubt concerning it.

18. What question did the author of Ecclesiastes raise in Ecclesiastes 3:21?

19. What analogy does Job use that expresses a similar fear in Job 14:7–10?

20. As Job is lamenting, what two pleas does he make in Job 14:13?

21. Showing the value of the lament, this now leads to a question on the part of Job. Find it in Job 14:14a.

22. God's Spirit now speaks to Job, giving him answers, hope, and confidence.

   a. What knowledge is Job given in Job 14:14b, and what does he resolve?

   b. What will God do and why, according to Job 14:15?

   c. The truth of Job 14:15 was beautifully illustrated when Jesus called forth Lazarus from the tomb (John 11). He loved Lazarus, wept when he died, and called for "the creature [his] hands had made." He feels the same about you. How does this truth help you to face death with confidence?

   d. How does the second verse of "Abide with Me, My Redeemer" echo this truth?

   e. What will God remember and what will He forget, according to Job 14:16?

   f. What will He do with our sin, according to Job 14:17?

   g. How is this different from what Job's "friends" and the enemy are telling him?

DAY 5: HOLD THOU THY CROSS BEFORE MY CLOSING EYES

Before Beginning Your Private Study, Sing:

Sing all of "Abide with Me, My Redeemer" along with Amy.

Study:

So often we do not know the reason why we suffer. But this we *do* know: it is not because God doesn't care. Of all the world religions only Christianity has a God who entered into our suffering; the cross helps us to accept the mystery.

God never gives Job the reason he suffered. *We* know, because we are privy to the interchange between Satan and God, but God never tells Job about this conversation. If He had, that would have nullified the wager, for if Job knew that he was going to be used to encourage countless sufferers in the future, then he would have had a reason to put up with it beyond simply loving God. Job had to suffer and not know why—and sometimes we do too.

Throughout the book, Job pleads for an audience with God. At the close, God grants Job his request. Throughout the book, the name used for God has been *Elohim*, the impersonal force, the Creator. But now, in Job 38, for the first time, this changes. Now the Hebrew word translated "Lord" is *Yahweh*, the personal Savior. This is the God who is going to suffer for Job, who is going to die and pay the highest price for Job's redemption. And this very caring and personal God is entering into dialogue with Job. When God talked to Satan, a Hebrew word is used that connotes a one-way conversation. But now, the word *answered* is a Hebrew word that connotes dialogue.

I see a pattern in Scripture and in life—when a child of God questions God, God's most frequent form of dialogue is to ask a question in return. God doesn't explain or defend Himself, but helps us remember who we are and who He is—and, in so doing, to simply trust His wisdom and sovereignty.

23. How does God come to Job, and what is His first statement in Job 38:1–3?

★24. Read Job 38–39 and write down a few of the poetic questions that stand out to you. What is God really asking Job to remember?

★25. What question does God ask Job in Job 40:8? How is this prophetic?

26. Read the final chapter of Job.

    a. In Job 42:1–6, how does Job respond to God?

    b. How does God deal with Job's "friends"?

27. Is there a difficult mystery in your life with which you need to trust God?

28. If you read chapter 8 of the book *The God of All Comfort*, what stood out to you?

29. What will you remember about this week's lesson? How could you apply it?

GROUP PRAYER TIME

Circle in groups of three and four for conversational prayer. Begin with praise, using some of the promises and passages from Job. Then individually lift up a personal concern to the Lord, and allow the others to support you.

Jesus, Lover of My Soul*

Jesus, lover of my soul, let me to Thy bosom fly,
While the nearer waters roll, while the tempest still is high.
Hide me, O my Savior, hide, till the storm of life is past;
Safe into the haven guide; O receive my soul at last.

Other refuge have I none, hangs my helpless soul on Thee;
Leave, ah! leave me not alone, still support and comfort me.
Hide me, O my Savior, hide, till the storm of life is past;
Safe into the haven guide; O receive my soul at last.

All my trust on Thee is stayed, all my help from Thee I bring;
Cover my defenseless head with the shadow of Thy wing.

O what grace with Thee is found, grace to cover all my sin;
Let the healing streams abound; make and keep me pure within.
Hide me, O my Savior, hide, till the storm of life is past;
Safe into the haven guide; O receive my soul.
Safe into the haven guide; O receive my soul at last.

Words by: Charles Wesley, 1740
Music by: Joseph Parry, 1879
Arr. by: Amy S. Wixtrom and Gary Wixtrom, 1998 and 2009
©2009 G. B. WIX Publishing ASCAP

* Available on the companion music CD

MY HEART IS STIRRED

(Hymn: "Jesus, Lover of My Soul")

CHARLES WESLEY WROTE 6,500 HYMNS, BUT "JESUS, LOVER OF MY SOUL" HAS OFTEN BEEN considered the best, in a close race with "Hark, the Herald Angels" and "O for a Thousand Tongues to Sing." His brother John considered "Jesus, Lover of My Soul" too sentimental, as many left-brained theologians might. But, oh! Charles is writing about *the heart* of Christianity —for Christianity is not about being a good person, but about having your heart stirred and transformed by the Lover of your soul. We've looked at many melodious sonnets, but of all of them, I believe the picture of Jesus as our Lover, as our Bridegroom, as the One who woos, wins, and weds, is the one that can transform our hearts like no other. It certainly has transformed my heart.

This classic hymn is certainly one for times of trouble; if ever we needed to know that Jesus is for us, that He loves us fiercely, it is when we are in the storms of life. If we don't believe that, *our* love will grow cold and we will let go of our only lifeline, sinking to the depths of the icy ocean.

ICEBREAKER

Think about a love story or a romantic rescue that moved your heart, and then look deeper. How can you glimpse Jesus in it? (If you can't come up with your own, how can you see Him in *Sleeping Beauty*, *Pride and Prejudice*, *Miss Potter*, or *Redeeming Love*?)

DAY 1: LOVER OF MY SOUL

Before Beginning Your Study, Sing:

Using the CD, sing along with Amy's version of "Jesus, Lover of My Soul." Think about the words, the plaintive pleas, the "o" and "ou" sounds so common to a lament.

Study:

Pastor Joe Coffey of Hudson (Ohio) Community Chapel has said, "The Bible begins with a wedding in Genesis, ends with a wedding in Revelation, and is shot through with pictures of a faithful Bridegroom and an unfaithful bride."[1] The Bible is *one* story of a great Hero who came from heaven to rescue His bride. When Kathy Troccoli and I wrote three study guides on "Falling in Love with Jesus," we still were not able to cover all the pictures in Scripture of this ultimate Bridegroom. Today we will glimpse just a few so you can see how scriptural it is to regard Jesus as the Lover of your Soul.

1. In the book of Ruth, hidden in Boaz—the man who rescues Naomi and Ruth—is Jesus, "the Kinsman-Redeemer" Bridegroom.

   ⋆a. How can you see Him in Ruth 2:8–9?

   ⋆b. How can you see Him in Ruth 3:9–11?

   c. Name one way the Lover of Your Soul has protected you, provided for you, or rescued you.

2. In the Song of Songs, the story of a king's love for a peasant maiden is also an allegory for the love of King Jesus for you and for me. Charles Spurgeon says, "We see Jesus in every book of the Bible, but it is in the Song of Songs that we see His heart for us."[2] How do you see His heart for you in the following:

*a. Though the maiden feels ashamed in the king's presence (Song of Songs 1:6), how does he see her? (2:2) What analogy do you see?

*b. How does the king lavish the maiden with love in Song of Songs 2:4?

c. Name one time Jesus lavished love on you.

d. By the close of the Song of Songs, what is the maiden doing though she has been through the desert? (8:5)

e. What similarity do you see between the maiden "leaning on her lover" and the opening lines of "Jesus, Lover of My Soul"?

f. Share a time when hardship caused you to either lean into the Lover of Your Soul or back away from Him.

The world often thinks of Christianity in terms of embracing a certain morality—but unlike other world religions, Christianity is about a relationship, a relationship with the Lover of Our Souls. Unless you understand this, you do not understand Christianity. In John Wesley's famous words describing his conversion, unless "your heart has been strangely warmed," unless you have been captivated by the Lover of Your Soul, you may not be a Christian at all.

3. Read Psalm 45.

   a. Describe the psalmist's emotions in verse 1.

   b. Read the description of our ultimate Bridegroom coming back for us in Psalm 45:2–8. What pictures or metaphors stand out to you? Why?

   c. What statement is made in verse 10? Why, do you think?

DAY 2: WHILE THE TEMPEST STILL IS HIGH

Before Beginning Your Study, Sing:

Memorize the first verse of "Jesus, Lover of My Soul." (Choose Amy's or the traditional lyrics.) Then sing the second verse reflectively.

Study:

This is clearly a hymn for danger, a pleading for our souls to be brought safely into God's haven. What is vital to comprehend is that our greatest danger, always, is not earthly but eternal—the danger of our love growing cold. We are often so earthbound in our vision that we think of danger as threatening our health or wealth or earthly treasures. As a family, we had to shift in our thinking from the earthly to the eternal. Steve asked us to pray more for his soul than his body, and so we did. That was the *real* battle, a battle God won for Steve and for us.

On a warm spring day this year I sat on the grass with my family and heard Sara Groves share and sing at an outdoor concert. Before singing "Song for My Sons," written for her still-small children, she explained the inspiration for her lyrics:

> I think my sons and my new daughter will face things that I can't even comprehend. And that evil, that darkness, that hurt will make them want to shut their hearts. Even now believers are shutting up their hearts and they're closing the windows and locking the doors. But Jesus says, "I want you to keep your door open in the face of terrorism, in the face of all the ills that the world has to offer. I want you to keep your heart open and love your God and love your neighbor."[3]

(You can listen to part of "Song for My Sons," or purchase it, on iTunes.)

4. Read Matthew 24:3–13.

    a. To what does Jesus compare wars, earthquakes, and famines in the end times ? (v. 8) What do you know about birth pains and how they work? What does this teach you?

    b. What will follow the increase of these calamitous events, according to Matthew 24:9?

c. The two greatest commands are to love God and to love one another. How will these be disobeyed, and why, according to Matthew 24:10?

d. What else will happen, according to Matthew 24:11?

*e. What are some of the false teachings we are hearing within churches concerning suffering?

f. Write out Matthew 24:12 below to help you look at it more closely.

g. What truths can you speak to your soul to help keep your love from growing cold in hard times? Write them concisely here.

> Jesus, lover of my soul, let me to Thy bosom fly,
> While the nearer waters roll, while the tempest still is high.
> Hide me, O my Savior, hide, till the storm of life is past;
> Safe into the haven guide; O receive my soul at last.

DAY 3: OTHER REFUGE HAVE I NONE

Before Beginning Your Study, Sing

Memorize the second verse of "Jesus, Lover of My Soul." Sing the first and second verses by heart, and the third looking at the lyrics.

Study:

Though Satan wants us to believe we cannot trust God, but should run to "other lovers" for comfort and help, Wesley knew the only place where true safety can be found is in the bosom of Jesus.

It breaks God's heart when we run to other lovers, not only because He is forgotten, but because when we do, our very souls are in peril. God gave us the story of Hosea to help us understand how we break His heart and imperil our souls when we look for love in all the wrong places.

5. How is Hosea's unfaithful bride described in each of the following verses?

a. Hosea 2:5

b. Hosea 2:8

c. Hosea 2:13b

6. Because Hosea's bride will not listen, what does the Lord do in Hosea 2:14–17? What is His purpose for "leading her into the desert"?

7. When you face the deserts of suffering, loneliness, and stress, where do you run? What can you learn from the passages you studied in questions 5 and 6?

8. When we run to people, food, immorality, or any other temporary haven, we begin to move in a downward spiral. Trace this downward spiral in Romans 1:18–32, finding a reference that shows:

   a. How, though people knew God existed, they did not thank or glorify Him

   b. How they worshiped what God made instead of God Himself

   c. How God gave them over to their lusts

   d. How God gave them over to a depraved mind

e. How they approved of immorality in others

9. What warning can you find from this passage for not letting your love grow cold?

Other refuge have I none, hangs my helpless soul on Thee;
Leave, ah! leave me not alone, still support and comfort me.
Hide me, O my Savior, hide, till the storm of life is past;
Safe into the haven guide; O receive my soul at last.

DAY 4: WITH THE SHADOW OF THY WING

Before Beginning Your Study, Sing:
Memorize the third verse of "Jesus, Lover of My Soul." Sing the first three verses.

Study:
I'm not giving away Steve's trench coat. I want to see it when I open the closet. I want to run my hand through its soft furry lining. If I have to run up to our mailbox in the rain, it's that trench coat I reach for—a sheltering shield covering me from head to foot, protecting me from the wet, yet flooding my heart with memories—like the cold day he introduced himself to me on the campus of Northwestern University. We were standing in front of the library and I was shivering. Suddenly he took off his coat and wrapped it around my shoulders. My knees nearly buckled.

Why do these memories of Steve in his trench coat warm my heart? Why do I love the romantic movies that have a man, often in a trench coat, racing to rescue a woman in the rain? (*Breakfast at Tiffany's*, *The Sound of Music*, *Sleepless in Seattle*, *Miss Potter* . . .) Because I am reminded of Jesus, the Lover of my soul, the One who will either stop the storm or will cover me with His wing, keeping me warm and safe until it has passed.

The word picture we are going to study, beginning today, is found in this line of "Jesus, Lover of My Soul":

Cover my defenseless head with the shadow of Thy wing

The Hebrew word *kanaph* is translated in many different ways—as "shade," as "shadow," as "wing," as a "garment" that covers one stripped of covering. Its connotation is personal and tender: like a mother bird sheltering her young with her wing; like a father wrapping his shivering little girl in a blanket; like a husband who takes off his coat to shield his wife from the rain. In medieval Jewish wedding ceremonies, the groom took off his prayer shawl and covered his bride as a symbol of his willingness to tenderly cover her with protection, provision, and love. Hosea covered Gomer with his robe when she stood naked to be sold on the auction block. *Kanaph* represents rescue—tenderly protecting and providing for one in need.

10. What picture of covering is given in each of the following passages? (Don't rush—for you are walking past poignant portraits that can penetrate your heart for storms ahead.)

   a. In biblical days, widows were truly destitute unless a man in the family "covered" them with protection and provision. In Ruth 3, at the urging of her mother-in-law, Naomi, Ruth goes in the night to Boaz, their close relative. What does she say to him in Ruth 3:9? Again, try to visualize this and put it in your own words.

> The word *kanaph* in the above may be translated "corner," "skirt," "covering," or "wing."

   b. Ezekiel 16:4–14 paints an allegorical picture of the great love and care that God has shown for His people from the beginning. How did God repeatedly care for and "cover" them?

> The word *kanaph* in the above passage occurs in verse 8 and may be translated "corner of my garment."

c. A more tranquil picture of *kanaph* is found in Song of Songs 2:3, possibly translated "shade." What do you see?

d. Perhaps the most famous picture, and the one we see most clearly in "Jesus, Lover of My Soul" is in Psalm 91:1–6. Try to visualize this image and put it in your own words.

> The word *kanaph* in the above is translated "wings" in most Bible translations.

11. Summarize what you've learned from today's word pictures concerning the Lord's *kanaph*: His love, care, and protection.

> All my trust on Thee is stayed, all my help from Thee I bring;
> Cover my defenseless head with the shadow of Thy wing.
> O what grace with Thee is found, grace to cover all my sin;
> Let the healing streams abound; make and keep me pure within.

12. Sing the third verse of "Jesus, Lover of My Soul" again. Do you see or hear anything you didn't before?

DAY 5: HIDE ME, O MY SAVIOR, HIDE

Before Beginning Your Study, Sing:

Memorize the rest of "Jesus, Lover of My Soul." Sing it all.

You may want to listen to a few other versions of this hymn. Indelible Grace and Hillsong both have contemporary renditions. Sara Groves' song 'Hiding Place" contains the words from Psalm 32, which we will study today. (All are available through iTunes.)

Study:

One of the surest ways to send Satan fleeing is honest, soul-felt confession to the Lord. Often we *do* look for love in all the wrong places, but when we come to Him in true repentance, sorrowful and willing to do the U-turn, He is faithful and just to forgive us. The psalm you will study today is a penitential psalm of David, filled with word pictures to penetrate our hearts and revive our passion.

13. In what context does Psalm 32:1 use the picture of covering?

14. Meditate on Psalm 32:2.

    a. What does this verse say?

    b. How can confession and forgiveness keep us from deceiving ourselves and others?

15. Find the parallelism in Psalm 32:3–4.

16. How is the word *cover* used in Psalm 32:5? What is the connection with how it is used in verse 1 ("Blessed is he ... whose sins are covered")?

Take a moment in your own time with God to uncover your sins to Him and ask Him for forgiveness.

17. What is the word picture in Psalm 32:6? Find similar phrasing in "Jesus, Lover of My Soul."

18. Describe the word pictures in Psalm 32:7.

19. What "songs of deliverance" have become particularly meaningful to you? Why?

20. What word pictures can you find in Psalm 32:9?

21. What reason is given in verse 10 for being responsive to the Spirit?

22. What three commands are given in verse 11? Are you improving in these? Explain.

23. If you read chapter 9 of the book *The God of All Comfort*, what do you remember?

24. What will you remember from this lesson and why?

GROUP PRAYER TIME

Circle in groups of three and four for conversational prayer. Begin by sharing any storm you are currently experiencing, and ask the others to pray that your love will not grow cold now or in the future. Pray for one another's children or spiritual children—that their love will not grow cold as lawlessness increases. Close by singing together the first verse of "Jesus, Lover of My Soul."

WHAT WONDROUS LOVE*

What wondrous love is this, O my soul, O my soul!
What wondrous love is this, O my soul!
What wondrous love is this, that caused the Lord of bliss
To bear the dreadful curse for my soul, for my soul,
To bear the dreadful curse for my soul.

When I was sinking down, sinking down, sinking down,
When I was sinking down, sinking down,
When I was sinking down, beneath God's righteous frown,
Christ laid aside His crown for my soul, for my soul,
Christ laid aside His crown, for my soul.

To God and to the Lamb, I will sing, I will sing,
To God and to the Lamb, I will sing.
To God and to the Lamb who is the great "I Am";
While millions join the theme, I will sing, I will sing;
While millions join the theme, I will sing.

And when from death I'm free, I'll sing on, I'll sing on;
And when from death I'm free, I'll sing on.
And when from death I'm free, I'll sing and joyful be;
And through eternity, I'll sing on, I'll sing on;
And through eternity, I'll sing on.

WORDS ATTRIBUTED TO: ALEXANDER MEANS
MUSIC BY: WILLIAM WALKER, 1835
ARR. BY: AMY S. WIXTROM AND GARY WIXTROM, 1995
©1995 G. B. WIX PUBLISHING ASCAP

* Available on the companion music CD

GOD HAS NOT
HIDDEN HIS FACE

(Hymn: "What Wondrous Love")

"WHAT WONDROUS LOVE" IS PART OF THE RICH MUSIC HERITAGE OF APPALACHIA—ONE OF MANY songs the poorest of the poor in America sang to give themselves hope. Think of coal mining families, eking out an existence, trying to feed and clothe many children, living in run-down shacks, and often dying young. Life was hard, but plaintive melodies flowed through those beautiful tree-covered mountains, helping the people hold onto God, beauty, and their roots. Traditional Appalachian music was mostly based upon Anglo-Celtic folk ballads, often sung unaccompanied, and usually by women, who served as keepers of their families' culture.

Bobbie Wolgemuth reflects on these mountain people and the melodies and lyrics that were passed on through the generations:

> These plain folks maintained the memory and the meaning of their faith by singing. They knew well the art of connecting with one another, whether hunting on the ridge, quilting together with neighbors, or shelling lima beans on the back porch with their families.[1]

My husband loved these Appalachian ballads. One of his favorite movies was *Coal Miner's Daughter*. The only song he requested at his funeral was "Waitin' on the Far Side Banks of Jordan," written by Terry Smith and sung by June Carter Cash to Johnny when she was dying. I cannot listen to it without weeping, for it tells of Steve waiting and watching for me, and, when he sees me coming, running across the shallow water and reaching for my hand.

William Walker, who first put "What Wondrous Love" into a collection in the early 1800s, discovered it in his travels around southern Appalachia. There are many versions of the song offered by iTunes, by artists ranging from Jars of Clay to the National Philharmonic. But personally, I think Amy Shreve's pure lilting voice and Celtic harp best captures its heritage.

ICEBREAKER

Are you listening to music differently or singing more than before you began this study? If so, share something about it.

DAY 1: To Bear the Dreadful Curse for My Soul

Before Beginning Your Study, Sing:

Listen to Amy's version of "What Wondrous Love" on the CD. Musician Bobbie Wolgemuth points out that the music "takes us down to the sinking places with minor-sounding tones and then lifts us up with the hope of eternity through the words. Like pieces of scraps sewn together to tell a story, this hymn is a beautiful patchwork of folk art."[2]

Study:

Though life can be hard, and certainly was for the people in Appalachia, God has not hidden His face. He bore the dreadful curse for our souls.

Reflect on this opening verse:

> What wondrous love is this, O my soul, O my soul!
> What wondrous love is this, O my soul!
> What wondrous love is this that caused the Lord of bliss
> To bear the dreadful curse, for my soul, for my soul,
> To bear the dreadful curse, for my soul.

1. As in many laments, the singer is talking to her soul. What is she telling her soul in this verse?

> If you find these next questions challenging,
> do your best before looking at the study notes!

*2. Often, in times of suffering, we can think we are not loved by God. Yet the cross shows us at once how bad we are and yet how loved we are. Find each of these truths in the lyrics on page 174.

*3. Close your eyes and listen, reflecting on the sounds in this verse: the words ending in "s" sounds, and their relationship, as well as the plaintive, repetitive "o" and "ou" sounds. How does the minor key augment them? What do you hear?

4. Many church people, indeed, many who may even be Christians, think that Christianity is about living a good life. Their worldview is that good people follow the morals of Christianity and that unbelievers do not. But that isn't what the Bible tells us. In Romans 3, Paul is talking to God's people (the Jews) and telling them that they have the same problem as the "outsiders" (the Gentiles). We need this message just as much today. Read Romans 3:9–24.

a. What question and answer do you find in verse 9?

b. In the list of evidences of our depravity found in verses 10–18, name one that has been true of you.

c. Can we become good by following moral laws? What do verses 19–20 tell us?

d. Who has sinned, according to verse 23?

e. What then is our hope, according to verse 24?

★f. How do you find this truth in the first verse of "What Wondrous Love"?

The cross at once reveals how bad we are (for He had to die for us), yet how loved we are (for He did die). Sing the first verse of "What Wondrous Love" in praise to Him.

DAY 2: WHEN I WAS SINKING DOWN

Before Beginning Your Study, Sing:

Begin learning the lyrics of "What Wondrous Love." The repetition makes them fairly easy to learn—so work on the first two verses today.

Study:

The psalms often use the metaphor of drowning or "sinking down into the mire" to describe our helplessness—both our inability to save ourselves from God's wrath, and also the help-lessness we feel when we receive catastrophic news. When I learned that Steve had cancer, I certainly felt like I was drowning. Yet looking back, I realize that God was on His way. I am riveted by the poetic imagery in Psalm 18. Just like the psalmist, I felt "the cords of death en-tangling me." But God heard and "the earth trembled and mountains shook" as He parted the heavens to come down, mounting the cherubim and flying on the wings of the wind to His child:

> He reached down from on high and took hold of me;
> he drew me out of deep waters.
>
> PSALM 18:16

5. Read Psalm 40:1–3.

    a. What word picture does the psalmist use to describe his great need for salvation? Can you identify? If so, share something about it.

    b. What word picture does the psalmist use for the change? Who did it?

    c. What else did God give him, according to verse 3? Why?

    d. How do you see the message of Psalm 40:1–2 paralleled in the second verse of "What Wondrous Love"?

6. Read Psalm 69:1–3. How does the psalmist describe himself?

7. Read Psalm 69:13–18 and list at least five requests the psalmist makes of God.

8. In Psalm 69:17 the psalmist asks God not to hide His face. We know God is too pure to look on sin, so why it is it that we can still ask Him not to hide His face from us?

> When I was sinking down, sinking down, sinking down,
> When I was sinking down, sinking down,
> When I was sinking down beneath God's righteous frown,
> Christ laid aside His crown, for my soul, for my soul,
> Christ laid aside His crown, for my soul.

9. Consider the second verse once more. Do you have any new thoughts or observations about it? If so, share.

DAY 3: TO GOD AND TO THE LAMB, WHO IS THE GREAT "I AM"

Before Beginning Your Study, Sing:

Sing the first two verses of "What Wondrous Love" without notes and learn the third verse.

Study:

Shortly before Steve's diagnosis, our daughter Sally was going through her own intense private suffering. She was asking, "Why?" God spoke to her miraculously, and, in so doing, also comforted us.

Sally is an artist, and when she had an art show at the Francis Schaeffer Institute in St. Louis, one of her paintings was of Aslan, the great lion who represents Jesus in C. S. Lewis's Chronicles of Narnia. She painted him standing, regally, in the wind. The painting had been sold, but Sally received many commissions to do more paintings of Aslan. She began working on her first commission the summer Steve was diagnosed. Because Sally was struggling with the question: "How could a good God allow all this evil and suffering in the world?" she hoped this painting would help give her the answer. She was intrigued by this passage from *The Lion, the Witch, and the Wardrobe*:

> "Who is Aslan?" asked Susan.
>
> "Aslan?" said Mr. Beaver. "Why, don't you know? He's the King . . ."
>
> "Is—is he a man?" asked Lucy.
>
> "Aslan a man!" said Mr. Beaver sternly. "Certainly not. I tell you he is the King of the wood and the son of the great Emperor-beyond-the-Sea. Don't you know who is the King of beasts? Aslan is a lion—*the* Lion, the great Lion."
>
> "Ooh!" said Susan. "I'd thought he was a man. Is he—quite safe?"...
>
> "Safe?" said Mr. Beaver ... "Who said anything about safe? 'Course he isn't safe. But he's good. He's the King, I tell you."[3]

"How," Sally asked, "could Jesus be both not safe and good?" Sally believed that in the artistic process, the Holy Spirit could help her paint a good but unsafe lion, though she herself did not know how to do it.

Monday, July 7
Twenty-five days before Steve's diagnosis

Sally has purchased a huge canvas, because, as she says, "Aslan needs to be big." She's watching National Geographic videos of lions, and pouring over photographs of lions. Tomorrow she will begin.

Monday, July 14
Eighteen days before Steve's diagnosis

Sally's been going to her studio each day, for most of the day, praying for You to work through her. Then she throws down globs of paint, in the manner of Jackson Pollock, and shapes those globs with her pallet knife, asking You to guide her.

Tuesday, July 21
Eleven days before Steve's diagnosis

I crept up to the studio to look—dying to see. I'm so amazed at what is taking shape—the painting is more realistic than abstract, yet there are shadows and mysterious parts, as You are mysterious. Aslan's head is huge, with a wild mane, and a muscular body. He's stepping toward the viewer. But [Sally's] not happy when I praise it. "I've got the 'not safe' part—but where is the 'good' part?"

Sunday, July 27

Five days before Steve's diagnosis

Sally finished her painting. It's a beautiful painting, but it didn't give her the answer she hoped for. She brought it to church to display.

Then something amazing happened.

A lady came up behind Sally and said, "Sally—do you see the other animal in this painting?"

Sally thinks people see all kinds of things in abstract art, but she was gracious. "Tell me what you see."

"I see a lamb," the woman said. Then she took her finger and outlined it.

As Sally explains,* "This was no vision in the clouds. I could really see it. There, right under Aslan's face, at his heart, was a lamb. I could hardly believe I hadn't seen it. It looked like it had been bound, its legs tied. Like in Revelation [5:5–6] when it says: 'Do not weep! See the Lion of the tribe of Judah.... And then I saw a Lamb, looking as if it had been slain.'"

Sally had her answer. At least, she knew what the answer to evil and suffering is not. It is not that Jesus doesn't care. He so loved the world that He was willing to be the Lamb that was slain.

10. Let's look more closely at the phrase "to God and to the Lamb."

a. How does John the Baptist refer to Jesus and why in John 1:29?

★b. According to Hebrew tradition, a lamb was sacrificed each Passover (Luke 22:7). Why, then, at the Last Supper, at that Passover meal, did Jesus and the disciples have all the Passover foods *except* the lamb? (1 Corinthians 5:7)

c. Why, according to 1 Peter 1:19, was only Jesus qualified to be the Lamb?

*You can see this painting and a video about it on my website, www.deebrestin.com.

d. Why did the elders tell John not to weep in Revelation 5:4–5?

e. And when John looked again, who did he see? (5:6)

f. What significance do you see in the fact that Jesus is both Lion and Lamb?

g. What do you learn about the Lamb in Revelation 7:14–17?

h. What do you learn about Him in Revelation 17:14?

"What Wondrous Love" has such profound biblical truth. It makes me think of how there will be a great reversal one day, and those who had little status on this earth—like many in Appalachia where the song was birthed—may have great status in heaven, for God gives wisdom to the simple and elevates the humble. The pairing, for example, of "to God and to the Lamb" with "who is the Great I Am" is deeper than you might at first see. "To God and to the Lamb" is a reference to God the Father and to Jesus, but so is "the Great I Am."

The phrase "I Am" is actually a repetition of "I AM WHO I AM" (*ego eimi*). In both the Hebrew, and in the Septuagint, which is the Greek translation of the Hebrew, it is "I Am" twice.

★11. What question does Moses ask in Exodus 3:13–14, and how does God the Father respond? What reflections do you have on this name?

In Exodus, I AM refers to God the Father, but in the gospel of John, it refers to Jesus. There are eight times when Jesus uses the same phrase, which is literally "I AM, I AM." He says:

- I AM the Light of the world. (John 8:12)
- I AM the Bread of life. (John 6:35)
- I AM the Door. (John 10:7)
- I AM the Good Shepherd. (John 10:11)
- I AM the Resurrection and the Life. (John 11:25)
- I AM the Way, the Truth, and the Life. (John 14:6)
- I AM the Vine. (John 15:1)
- Before Abraham was, I AM. (John 8:58)

R. C. Sproul explains that these claims "are one of the purest unvarnished declarations of Deity that Jesus ever makes in the Scripture, and it was not missed by His audience, for they took up stones to stone Him."[4]

12. What claim does Jesus make in John 8:12, and how do the Pharisees respond?

13. Read the debate between Jesus and the Jews in John 8:31–59, and then find the main response of Jesus or the Jews in each of the following verses:

a. What does Jesus tell them in verse 31?

b. How do the Jews respond in verse 33?

c. What is Jesus' rebuttal in verse 34?

d. What else does Jesus say in verse 37?

e. How do the Jews respond in verse 39?

f. Find at least three things that Jesus accuses them of in verses 42–45.

g. What does Jesus tell them in verse 56?

h. How do they respond in verse 57?

i. What does Jesus say in verse 58?

j. How do they respond in verse 59?

14. Now write down your reflections on this line:

To God and to the Lamb, who is the great "I Am"

DAY 4: AND WHEN FROM DEATH I'M FREE

Before Beginning Your Study, Sing:

Sing the first three verses of "What Wondrous Love" without notes and learn the last verse.

Study:

Even the staunchest of believers may fear going through the death experience. The Bible says it is our last enemy, and it can feel formidable. Appalachian people faced death daily, for coal mining, malnutrition, and accompanying disease made them more vulnerable.

Steve often referred to death as "crossing the river." He loved John Bunyan's classic 1678 allegory, *The Pilgrim's Progress*. He read to our children from it and we owned many editions with beautiful illustrations. In fact, when I wrote a study guide on 1 Peter (*A Woman of Confidence*), Steve encouraged me to put some of those illustrations in it. One drawing Steve especially liked was of Christian and Hopeful finally arriving at the river to cross into the Celestial City. The water is cold, dark, and deep, the waves billowing. Christian is fearful, but Hopeful tells him that the "bottom is good." Christian's head is going under water, but Hopeful helps him stay afloat, reassuring him all the way, saying, "Be of good cheer, Jesus Christ maketh thee whole." Bunyan writes:

And with that Christian brake out with a loud voice, "Oh I see him again; and he tells me, 'When thou passest through the waters, I will be with thee; and through the rivers, they shall not overflow thee.'" Isa. 43:2. Then they both took courage, and the enemy was after that as still as a stone, until they were gone over.[5]

In the midst of our doubts and fears, the truth remains: "the bottom is good." The Solid Rock of Christ is steady. And one day we will be free of death, that last enemy.

And for those of us not yet free of death, we need to speak the truth to our soul—not only the truth that Christ will conquer the last enemy, but that heaven will not be some boring ethereal place we should fear, but, instead, the best of earth.

Thursday, June 14
Twenty months after Steve's death

At the cottage alone. Heartbreakingly beautiful sunset. I want Steve here to share it with me. To lie with me in the hammock, and to watch the crimson and violet rays of the sinking sun spread across the sky and bay. To have supper on the porch, play Scrabble, talk of great books, pray. I always dreamt that one day we'd have long sabbaticals here together writing.

I must accept it is never to be. Steve's not coming back.

But I will go to him. And heaven is not some ethereal place; it is as real as this, only better. I love what I'm learning from Your Word about heaven. You are constantly in the business of reforming. Everything You made is good, and You will reverse the effects of the fall. Heaven will be like the best of earth, only even better. Perhaps I will watch sunsets again with Steve and even watch this funny little badger waddle across the rocks. I'll hear Steve's great laugh again. I know we will have long conversations and never have to say good-bye again. He will be strong, healthy, and perfect. There will be no more sickness, no more death, and no more tears.

That's the truth, O my soul.

There is much that is mysterious about heaven, but we do know we will have bodies like Jesus did—and He was able to walk, talk, hug, and eat fish on the beach with Peter. In her book *Heaven*, Joni Eareckson Tada articulates what many of us have felt—that Revelation's descriptions of golden cities and seas of glass were not appealing—but she knew in her heart she could trust God, and as she began to seek Him and understand this mystery, He did reveal truths that ignited her soul and gave her a desire for heaven. Likewise, Sara Groves has a song about heaven called "What Do I Know?" that comes to the same conclusion. Though she doesn't know about streets of gold or bright lights at the end of tunnels, she does know that "to be absent from the body is to be present with the Lord"—and from what she knows of Jesus, that should be very good.

God's pattern is not to destroy, but to reform. Everything He made is good, and instead of destroying, He makes it new again. I see this now in the descriptions of heaven—for rather than us going up to an ethereal place, heaven comes down to earth, reforming it! Our journey must be brief today, but I pray it will be eye-opening.

15. What is the last enemy that God will destroy, according to 1 Corinthians 15:26?

16. Read 1 Corinthians 15:35–57.

   a. What question is asked in verse 35?

   b. What analogy in verse 37 helps us understand the difference between our earthly bodies and our resurrected bodies?

   c. What other differences, according to verse 42, will there be between our earthly bodies and our resurrected bodies?

   d. In what ways is *your* earthly body frail? What does it mean to you that you will be set free of that? How will your loved ones who know the Lord be set free from particular physical weaknesses?

"One day no more bulging middles or balding tops. No varicose veins or crow's feet. No more cellulite or support hose. Forget the thunder thighs and highway hips. Just a quick leapfrog over the tombstone and it's the body you've always dreamed of."

JONI EARECKSON TADA[6]

★e. Who is the last Adam? What was His body like when He was resurrected? What does verse 49 tell us?

17. Read Revelation 21:1–7.

    a. Do we go up or does heaven come down, according to verse 2?

    b. What do you learn about heaven from verses 3–4?

    c. What will Jesus do with the earth, according to verse 5?

18. Paul quotes Isaiah in 1 Corinthians 2:9. Write out this short quote about heaven and any reflections you have on it.

> And when from death I'm free, I'll sing on, I'll sing on;
> And when from death I'm free, I'll sing on.
> And when from death I'm free, I'll sing and joyful be . . .

DAY 5: I'll Sing On, I'll Sing On

Before Beginning Your Study, Sing:

Sing all of "What Wondrous Love."

Study:

The most frequent positive command in the Scripture is to sing or to praise. The most frequent negative command is to not fear. Do you see the connection?

I pray you have been blessed by this study and Amy's CD. If you liked this study, you may enjoy a similar one I did entitled *A Woman of Worship*, with the CD by Integrity Music. I would love to hear from you![7]

Please, sing on!

19. Sing what you can of "It Is Well with My Soul." Review lesson one and write down one thing you would like to remember from it.

20. Sing what you can of "Psalm 131." Review lesson two and write down one thing you would like to remember from it.

21. Sing what you can of "Come Thou Fount." Review lesson three and write down one thing you would like to remember from it.

22. Sing what you can of "O the Deep, Deep Love of Jesus." Review lesson four and write down one thing you would like to remember from it.

23. Sing what you can of "Be Thou My Vision." Review lesson five and write down one thing you would like to remember from it.

24. Sing what you can of "Be Still, My Soul." Review lesson six and write down one thing you would like to remember from it.

25. Sing what you can of "A Mighty Fortress." Review lesson seven and write down one thing you would like to remember from it.

26. Sing what you can of "Abide With Me, My Redeemer." Review lesson eight and write down one thing you would like to remember from it.

27. Sing what you can of "Jesus, Lover of My Soul." Review lesson nine and write down one thing you would like to remember from it.

28. Sing what you can of "What Wondrous Love." Review lesson ten and write down one thing you would like to remember from it.

29. What was your favorite hymn and why?

GROUP PRAYER TIME

Circle in small groups and have a time of praise, using lyrics from these hymns as springboards. Add to one another's sentences, and when there is a pause, have someone else bring up a new thought.

NOTES

LESSON ONE: The Cords of Death Entangled Me

1. T. M. Moore, *Ecclesiastes* (Downers Grove, Ill.: InterVarsity Press, 2001), 55.

2. Tim Keller, from the sermon series "Job: A Path through Suffering," www.redeemer.com.

3. Joseph Bayly, *The View from a Hearse* (Elgin, Ill.: David C. Cook, 1969), 40–41.

LESSON TWO: I Have Quieted My Soul

1. John D. Witvliet, *The Biblical Psalms in Christian Worship* (Grand Rapids: Eerdmans, 2007), xiii. St. Basil was a fourth-century bishop of Caesera, who was persecuted for the faith and known for his virtue; Dietrich Bonhoeffer was martyred for his part in a conspiracy to kill Hitler; and Bono is a contemporary Irish rock musician who has raised great amounts of money for combating starvation and AIDS in third world countries.

2. Lyrics by Annie S. Hawks, music by Robert Lowry, 1872. Public domain. Many versions of this are available on iTunes. Another, which is my particular favorite, is the version by Indelible Grace.

3. Philip Yancey, *The Bible Jesus Read* (Grand Rapids: Zondervan, 1999), 109.

4. Psalm 22:1b.

5. William Brown, *Seeing the Psalms* (Louisville, Ky.: Westminster John Knox, 2002), 2.

6. Ibid.

7. Psalm 77:2.

8. Psalm 6:3, 6.

9. "I Need Thee Every Hour," Hawks and Lowry.

10. Derek Kidner, *Psalms 73–150*, Tyndale Old Testament Commentaries (Downers Grove, Ill.: InterVarsity Press, 1973), 446.

LESSON THREE: Songs in the Night

1. Leonard Bernstein, *The Joy of Music* (New York: Simon and Schuster, 2004), 105.

2. C. S. Lewis, *Reflections on the Psalms* (New York: Harcourt, Brace, and World, 1958), 3.

3. Ephesians 5:19; Colossians 3:16.

4. The *Reformation Study Bible* debates that this phrase refers to three kinds of psalms, saying: "This restriction appears, however, to miss the point. He piles up the terms to highlight the wide range of musical expression that grateful and heartfelt praise to God calls forth from the body of Christ." R. C. Sproul, ed., *The Reformation Study Bible* (Nashville: Thomas Nelson, 1995), 1891.

5. John Stott, *The Letters of John* (Grand Rapids: Eerdmans, 2000), 99.

LESSON FOUR: Deep Calls to Deep

1. Luci Shaw, "The Need To Pay Attention: Darkness, Light, and the Visionary Eye," *Weavings* 16, no. 4, July/August, 2001, 21–22.

2. William P. Brown, *Seeing the Psalms* (Louisville, Ky.: Westminster John Knox, 2002), ix–x.

3. Tim Keller, "Lord of the Storm," sermon preached on March 3, 2006 at Redeemer Presbyterian Church, New York City. Available at www.redeemer.com.

4. Brown, *Seeing the Psalms*, 134.

5. Ibid., 119.

6. John Bunyan (1628–1688), as quoted in Charles Spurgeon, *The Treasury of David*, vol. 1 (Peabody, Mass.: Hendrickson, 1988), 285.

Lesson Five: Why Are You Downcast, O My Soul?

1. See Psalm 16:4.

2. Joan Didion, *The Year of Magical Thinking* (New York: Vintage, 2006), 37.

3. Two resources in finding a good Christian counselor in your area are Focus on the Family and the American Association of Christian Counselors. You can contact both on the web.

Lesson Six: Be Still, My Soul

1. Sally Magnusson, *The Flying Scotsman* (New York: Quartet Books, New York, 1981), 175.

2. Joni Eareckson Tada and Steven Estes, *When God Weeps* (Grand Rapids: Zondervan, 1997), 56.

3. At the printing of this guide, this sermon can be downloaded at www.redeemer.com under free sermons, "Suffering and Tragedy."

4. Psalm 77:6.

5. Ezra 3:10–11.

6. Psalm 77:9.

7. Derek Kidner, *Psalms 73–150*, Tyndale Old Testament Commentaries (Downers Grove, Ill.: Inter Varsity Press, 1973), 278.

8. Hosea 2:17.

Lesson Seven: Though the Mountains Fall into the Sea

1. T. M. Moore, *A Mighty Fortress* (Ross-shire, Scotland: Christian Focus Publications, 2003), 6.

2. Hans J. Hillerbrand, ed., *The Reformation* (Grand Rapids: Baker, 1964), 91.

Lesson Eight: I Know My Redeemer Lives

1. Kenneth W. Osbeck, *Amazing Grace: 366 Inspiring Hymn Stories and Daily Devotions* (Grand Rapids: Kregel, 1990), 130.

2. The Rev. Ed Hird (Rector, St. Simon's Anglican Church, North Vancouver, British Columbia), "Rediscovering Handel's Messiah," *The Deep Cover Crier*, April, 1993.

3. Mike Mason, *The Gospel According to Job* (Wheaton, Ill.: Crossway, 1994), 216.

4. Ibid., 217–218.

Lesson Nine: My Heart Is Stirred

1. Joe Coffey, "Love, the Secret of Life," sermon preached November 11, 2007 at Hudson Community Chapel, Hudson, Ohio.

2. Charles Spurgeon, "Better than Wine," sermon preached in 1896. Spurgeon Online Archive.

3. Sara Groves speaking at Shawnee Mission Park in Kansas City for Christ Community Church, April 26, 2009.

Lesson Ten: God Has Not Hidden His Face

1. Joni Eareckson Tada, John MacArthur, Robert and Bobbie Wolgemuth, *What Wondrous Love Is This* (Wheaton, Ill.: Crossway, 2002), 30.

2. Ibid.

3. C. S. Lewis, *The Lion, the Witch, and the Wardrobe* (New York: Harper, 1950), 85–86.

4. R. C. Sproul, "Before Abraham Was, I AM," *Knowing Christ*, Cassette 6 (Orlando: Ligonier Ministries, 1999).

5. John Bunyan, *The Pilgrim's Progress*. Public domain. Online version.

6. Joni Eareckson Tada, *Heaven: Your Real Home* (Grand Rapids: Zondervan, 1995). This quote was taken from the large print edition (New York: Walker and Company), 35.

7. You can write Dee or participate in her blog at www.deebrestin.com. Her guide *A Woman of Worship* is available through her website or many others, such as Amazon.com and Christianbook.com.

TIPS FOR THE GROUP FACILITATOR

Your role as a discussion facilitator for the small group is a vital one. You are not a teacher, but your role is to help the members look into the Word, to share what they are learning, and to feel welcome in the group. Here are some common questions facilitators have.

What if we don't have enough time to discuss the lesson?

These lessons are designed to be completed in ninety minutes in a small group. (Not more than twelve people on the rolls.) If you don't have that much time, or your group is large, you may choose one of these options:

- Divide the group and appoint another facilitator.
- Divide the lessons into twenty weeks, doing the opening two days the first week and the last three days the second week.
- Skip some questions, but always answer the final question each week.

How should I incorporate the music?

You may choose to sing the hymn together, listen to the hymn, or have each person in the group do that on their own. You may want to bring a verse of a different version for them to hear or see. There are a few short videos suggested in the Study Notes. Much of this depends on your time and your particular group.

What keeps people coming back?

Research shows that the main reason people drop out of a group is because they don't feel others really care about them. Here are a few things you can do:

- Warmly greet each person who comes.
- Gather an email list so you can thank them for coming or let an absent person know they were missed.
- Affirm answers with a smile, nod, or brief, "Good," "That's interesting."
- Encourage group interaction through prayer partners, "secret sisters," or asking for members to call or write an absent member.
- Plan at least one social time outside of the meeting—a lunch out, a game night, a picnic in the park or in front of someone's fireplace!

What do I do if I have a monopolizer?

- Pray. Often people who talk too much have some deep hurts.
- During discussion, don't sit directly across from this person, but next to them, if possible. Eye contact encourages sharing.
- Ask, "What does someone else think?" "Can we hear from someone who hasn't shared?"
- If the problem persists, take him or her aside gently and ask for their help. Say something like, "You have shared some great things. I wish some of the other members would share so easily. Could you help them by just sharing on a few questions and allowing there to be pauses so they can gather courage to speak up?"

What if members are not doing their homework?

You might set up accountability partners for a few weeks, putting more mature members who are completing their work with less mature members. Ask them to help each other by checking on each other through email or phone, to see how they are doing. Pray about this as a group, for we influence one another enormously.

What if a group member breaks down and his or her grief seems to overwhelm the group?

Because of the subject of this study, this is likely to happen. It is important to comfort, to listen, to care—but also to realize that continually being diverted will be harmful to everyone. Listen for a few minutes, then ask the group to get around this person and pray for him or her in sentence prayers. Really pray. Then move on. And then check on him or her during the week.

STUDY NOTES

LESSON ONE: The Cords of Death Entangled Me

(Hymn: "It Is Well with My Soul")

Note to the Discussion Leader: If you are able to rent the movie Amazing Grace: Five Hymns that Changed the World *(not the William Wilberforce film of the same name), play the fifteen-minute story behind "It Is Well with My Soul" for the group. It may be available from Netflix.*

3. Both say trouble will come. Both promise that one day Christ will overcome.

4. Ecclesiastes 7:14a tells us to be happy when times are good and to realize when times are bad that God has made those days too. This verse is pointing to the sovereignty of God—controlling both the good and the bad, having a divine purpose for each. (This is the same theme of "It Is Well with My Soul.") T. M. Moore's paraphrase of Ecclesiastes 7:14 (see question 5) is particularly helpful. Look at that paraphrase and reflect: What are we to consider? Is it to figure out why suffering has occurred? Perhaps—but often we cannot. More likely, it is to consider who God is and why we should trust Him—and to consider what we can learn from this trial.

9.b. It is the Lord who first brings up Job. God is in control here, and He is only going to give Satan enough rope to hang himself. God knows Job's heart and knows what Satan does not know. Job is not a fraud. He really does love God for Himself; he will pass the test, and encourage sufferers for centuries to come.

9.d. Satan believes Job serves God, not because he loves God for Himself, but because he wants God's blessings.

12.a. The music for the phrase "when peace like a river attendeth my way" is gentle, having no great leaps, except for the light little ripple with "attendeth," one of only two polysyllabic words in the phrase.

12.c. The notes for "sorrows" go up and are elongated, like a sea billow. *Sorrow* is an onomatopoeia—the word, with long vowels, sounding like what it means.

16.b. The prowling lion always looks for the weak, the wounded, the easy prey. We are easy prey to Satan when we are suffering.

19.b. Taking away a coat in winter makes you feel colder. Pouring vinegar on soda makes it explode. We can actually make the grieving person feel worse by giving pat answers, solutions, and even Scripture verses. Though Scripture is true, there is a time to speak and a time to be silent. I wanted to give a swift karate kick to the person who quoted Romans 8:28 to me at Steve's funeral.

Lesson Two: I Have Quieted My Soul

(Psalm/Song: "Psalm 131")

7.c. Satan's question is less of a question and more of a smirk. He's trying to get Eve to doubt God's wisdom and character. He twists God's command (from *one* tree to *any* tree) and sarcastically asks, "Did He *really* say?" (implying that God is unreasonable). He wants Eve to doubt the goodness of God.

9.b. The gospel is "rescue"despite our unworthiness. Every other religion throws the drowning person a manual on "how to swim." But Christianity sends a rescuer to the drowning person.

12. Satan wants us to doubt God's love, and he often accuses and reminds us of past sin as evidence that we do not deserve God's love (which we don't!). But verse 4 reminds us that the record has been wiped clean, that God forgives, and, therefore, He is to be feared. The word *fear* obviously means something other than "terror" here; rather "gratitude," "respect," and "awe."

Lesson Three: Songs in the Night

(Hymn: "Come Thou Fount")

5.a. God is not the author of evil, but He will use evil spirits for His own purposes. He did it in Job, and He does it here with Saul. He allows Saul to be tormented. Why, we cannot be sure. We do know that suffering, according to Deuteronomy 8, humbles us and tests what is in our hearts. But God also shows mercy here, allowing His gift of music to soothe Saul.

5.c. Music varies in quality, and it is wise to look for music that is played and sung well, and to avail ourselves of the best. Both simple praise choruses and complex hymns have value, but complex music is an acquired taste. By taking the time to understand the lyrics and to listen with your heart and mind, you will acquire this taste and its soothing power will be unleashed on your soul. Do not neglect it because effort is required to appreciate it. Those whose steady diet is fast food suffer in the long run.

10.a.(1) Both Jeremiah 2:13 and John 4:13 mention a futile way to quench our thirst and God's way to quench it. Unless the Spirit of God the Father and God the Son wells up in us, we will have no desire to love Him, to sing praises to Him. We must pray for this fount to well up.

10.b.(1) In Hebrews 13:15, note the opening, "Through Jesus,"—for again, we cannot do this on our own, but He is eager to do it. As we become more intimate with Him, often through "the sacrifice of praise," He turns our hearts of stone into hearts of flesh. "The sacrifice of praise" is a particularly meaningful phrase for those in pain, for often we do not feel like singing, even a lament. A lament is easier, and a lament *is* a form of praise because we are going *to* God instead of *away* from Him.

10.c.(1) The key to a transformed life is setting your affections on Jesus, letting Him be "your life" because you really trust His love. If you think the cross—the gospel—is just about being saved from hell, you haven't truly grasped the gospel. Jesus longs to save us from so many other things—we make so many things "our life" other than Him because we don't really trust His love.

22.b. Hear from many. You may need to pave the way in being vulnerable.

23.b. So many think only in terms of salvation from hell, but it is so important to see that Christ's love as shown on the cross was meant to melt our hearts of stone, changing us to live for Him instead of ourselves, to "bind" our wandering hearts to Him.

LESSON FOUR: Deep Calls to Deep

(Hymn: "O the Deep, Deep Love of Jesus")

1.d. God is enthroned over the flood—He is King, He is Lord of all. Nothing happens that He has not allowed. He has not lost control.

1.e. He will give strength and peace in the midst of the storm. It is important to know that not only is He in control, as verse 10 tells us, but that He loves us, as verse 11 demonstrates.

6. Jonah was guilty. Jesus was innocent. Jonah ran away from rescuing the Ninevites. Jesus ran toward us.

15.a.b.c. The psalmist's only food has been his tears. Since his tears are coming day and night, he's not sleeping. He's isolated, for he remembers, with longing, the times he was in fellowship with other believers as they traveled, worshiping together.

Lesson Five: Why Are You Downcast, O My Soul?

(Hymn: "Be Thou My Vision")

2. The repeated exhortation "put your hope in God" (Psalm 42:5, 10; 43:5) can be found in the repeated phrase "be Thou my vision"—nothing else ("naught be all else"). Nothing else—not riches, not man's empty praise—only Jesus.

7. *Naught* means "nothing"—nothing else should be our foundation, our vision. *Save* here means "take everything, but leave me Jesus."

11.c. The Pharisees thought they could save themselves by following the Law. We can't do it—only Jesus can rescue us. In the same way, if we focus on anything else in life to "save us," to give us meaning—whether riches, the praise of other people, or our own strength—we are in trouble.

12.e. Salvation is both an event and a process. We are saved from the wrath of God when He brings us to repentance and trust in His atoning work, but being saved from the habits of sin and false objects of trust takes time.

12.f. As we become conformed to Jesus, our hearts grow richer in compassion. Instead of being dimly aware of people, we are acutely aware of their needs, their hurts, and we, like Jesus, are moved with compassion to respond.

14. We need light to have vision. In order for Christ to be our vision, it isn't enough to experience an answer to prayer during the day, or to have our spirit quickened by the Word in our quiet time with Him, but we must have His presence all throughout the day—*Thy presence my light.*

15. Riches I heed not *because* Jesus is my treasure. It is never enough to stop longing for a false god, for our longing will only increase unless we fill that void with the real God.

16. *High king of heaven* and *ruler of all.* This is a verse about God's sovereignty. Even in trouble (whatever befall), we still plead for Him to be our vision, for He is the High King, He is the Ruler of all.

Lesson Six: Be Still, My Soul

(Hymn: "Be Still, My Soul")

2.b. and 2.d. Stephen is talking to the priests. A priest was one who interceded between the people and God. But now Stephen is saying they were not needed, for we have access to God through Christ. In fact, the dying Stephen sees "heaven open!" So often, when someone rejects Christ, it is not intellectual, but emotional. Because He is the Cornerstone, it means we have to give up whatever false cornerstone we have built on—and that's frightening. For the priests it was their identity and life's occupation—for so many it is other things: career, family, or a licentious lifestyle. When we are "cut to the heart," we either respond in repentance or rage.

4.a. Monosyllabic words are firm, as when speaking firmly to a child who is having trouble calming down.

7.e. This is a beautiful picture of how Christ's love does not depend on our actions but on His character. He is resolved, as shown by His staccato commands: "Rise! Let us go!"

10.a. It begins with "I" words, describing the psalmist's distress. There seems to be a "dialogue" with the Holy Spirit, with the psalmist asking questions which lead to a partial answer. Then the psalm changes to "You" words, as his attention turns to the character of God.

13.b. I like the way the melody goes up, strengthens, and lingers with "confidence." It has the sense of soaring strength which "nothing can shake."

15.a. We will be eating, just as Jesus was able to eat fish.

15.b. God will destroy the shroud of death.

15.c. Death swallowed up; tears wiped away (Randy Alcorn thinks there may still be tears in heaven until all is completed—and that's why they are wiped away instead of gone); and disgrace removed.

15.d. Think about "sorrow forgot, love's purest joys restored." I think about how we will not be able to hurt each other anymore!

16.a. The new Jerusalem will come down! Heaven will come down and renew the earth.

16.b. The saints (true believers) of every tribe and nation who are in heaven will be joined to the saints of every tribe and nation still living on earth.

16.d. "I am making everything new!" Everything God made was good—the ocean, the earth, people—but all have been corrupted by sin, so all will be renewed, restored to their former beauty.

LESSON SEVEN: Though the Mountains Fall into the Sea

(Hymn: "A Mighty Fortress")

1.b. Even mountains can fall into the sea, though that seems hard to imagine. Even good marriages can end when suffering is intense or when one dies; even solid careers can end; even beautiful friendships can go bad. But there is One who will never betray us, never move away, and never die. Nothing can shake Him. He is a Mighty Fortress.

1.c. Often something beautiful, such as a talented child or a beautiful marriage, becomes the focus of our lives. But it is only God who cannot be shaken.

2.a. *Ancient foe*—music is slow, in minor key, formidable; vowel sound of "o" is sonorous, melancholy
Work us woe—*foe* and *woe* rhyme, as they should; monosyllables are firm, warning, heavy; more "o" sounds
His craft and pow'r are great—music continues slowly, heavily
And armed with cruel hate—*great* and *hate* rhyme, as they should
On earth is not his equal—ends with notes going very low, like the enemy himself

3. The enemy wants you to despair of God's love and back away from Him. We will study this idea more fully on Day 5.

6. *Doth ask who that may be?* A rhetorical question that seems, because the answer is so obvious, to show irritation. Beneath the surface I sense, *Do you really not know who is in charge? Do you really think He is going to let Satan win?*

7.d. Satan was convinced Job loved God for His blessings rather than God Himself. Take the blessings away, Satan thought, and Job would curse God. Yet Job said, "Though he slay me, yet will I trust him." Satan lost the wager and sufferers throughout all of time have been strengthened.

11. *Satan trying*   *God trumping*
devils *filled*   yet God has *willed*
threaten to *undo us*   yet truth to triumph *through us*
his rage we can *endure*   for lo, his doom is *sure*
Truth each time: God is always the Victor.

14. So often we find security in this world, but it will not sustain us—it is passing away. But "the Spirit and the gifts" are eternal. We might as well hold "goods and kindred" loosely, for they too are passing away.

20.d. The greatest gift is intimacy with the father, which he is rejecting. He doesn't love the father; he loves the father's stuff. It is the happiest day of his father's life, but the older son cannot rejoice, for he has to share the father's stuff.

LESSON EIGHT: I Know My Redeemer Lives

(Medley: "Abide with Me, My Redeemer")

Note to the Discussion Leader: If you can get a copy of the short music video of Nicole C. Mullen singing "Redeemer," it would be a good way to begin your small group. You can see it online if your group is small enough to circle around a laptop computer.

1.a. The qualities of a lament are these: the plaintive melody, the plea for help, and the honest expression of pain (darkness is deepening, helpers and comforts are fleeing).

2.b. They are telling Jesus Himself of their sadness that He is dead; they mention "the third day" when He told them many times that He was going to be raised on "the third day" (see, for instance, Matthew 17:23 and Luke 18:33), yet they still don't understand; and they are astonished at their women. (The actual medical term that Luke uses when the women came running means "the delirious talk of the very ill.")

6. Proverbs are general truths, not promises. Therefore, they cannot be applied to every situation, which Eliphaz is doing. That's why a proverb in the mouth of a fool can be a dangerous thing. Though we reap what we sow, you cannot turn that around and claim that *all* suffering is a result of immorality. One of the cruelest things to do to someone who is suffering is to assume that it is the result of sin when it's not obviously so. Only God knows. And Job makes a good point in Job 6:14: Even if consequences are a result of sin, when someone is despairing, it might not be the best timing to heap on the criticism.

7. If our piety is our confidence instead of God, we are all in deep trouble. Just as no one can be good enough to earn salvation, neither can anyone be good enough to avoid pain. Our hope must be in God's mercy, not in ourselves.

8. Read this chilling account out loud, imagining Eliphaz almost relishing it, like some enjoy the spine-tingling emotions produced by a horror movie. Eliphaz, unable to distinguish the voice of God from the voice of the enemy, attributes it to God. But there is darkness, chilling terror (unlike a holy fear), and a disembodied spirit that made his hair stand on end. This is not the Holy One. This is the lying spirit that slithers in to cause the suffering to despair of the Holy One.

10.c. The Spirit and the Word never disagree, for they have the same Author. How many times I've heard someone say that God led them to marry an unbeliever. It cannot be! If what they "heard" contradicts the Bible, they are not hearing the Spirit of God.

24. God is reminding Job that He knows what He is doing. For us to question the Creator of the universe is the height of arrogance. Just because we cannot figure out the reason for suffering does not mean God doesn't have one.

25. One day Jesus will be condemned so that we can be justified.

LESSON NINE: My Heart Is Stirred

(Hymn: "Jesus, Lover of My Soul")

1.a. As Boaz provided for Ruth and protected Ruth, so does Jesus.

1.b. As Boaz willingly covered Ruth with the corner of his garment (in Jewish wedding ceremonies that symbolizes protection and provision), so Jesus covers us with His garment of righteousness.

2.a. He sees her as a lily among thorns. God sees us as forgiven, as white as snow, because we are covered in the righteousness of His Son.

2.b. He brings her to his banqueting table and his banner over her is love. When you ask someone to dine with you, it is an invitation to a more intimate relationship. He is lavishing her with a fine meal (the best of earthly delights) and surrounding her with love.

4.e. It is often taught that if you live right, pray hard enough, and have enough faith, then you will be healed on earth, or your suffering will be taken away. God may do this, but many godly people, including Jesus and the disciples and many "of whom the world was not worthy" were not spared and even died martyrs' deaths. This false teaching leads us to feel either angry at God (for supposedly not keeping His promise) or angry at ourselves (for not doing it right)—and then it is easy for our love to grow cold.

Lesson Ten: God Has Not Hidden His Face

(Hymn: "What Wondrous Love")

2. Lyrics that show us how bad we are: *to bear the dreadful curse for my soul.* (Our rebellion against loving God led to a curse.)

   Lyrics that show us how loved we are: *What wondrous love is this that caused the Lord of bliss.* (Christ didn't have to do it, but His love for us compelled Him.)

3. "S" sounds are soft and "o" and "ou" sounds are lament-like, beginning this song in a reflective mood. The minor key adds to this mood.

4.f. Though we are all under a curse, our hope is in the wondrous love of Christ.

10.b. Christ would be the Lamb who would be sacrificed. He was crucified and died during the hours (nine o'clock in the morning to three o'clock in the afternoon) that the lambs were sacrificed on Passover.

11. God could not tell Moses, "I AM like _____" for God is not like anyone or anything. He could only say, "I AM WHO I AM."

16.e. Christ is the last Adam. When He was resurrected He had a real body that could walk, talk, and eat. It was also different, for He could walk through a door and ascend into heaven.

Dear Friend,

Thanks so much for using *The God of All Comfort Bible Study Guide*. It is my desire to help those in pain find their way through it and into the arms of God. Therefore, I've asked Amy Shreve to team up with me to bring this message to churches and conferences across North America. I've never heard anyone sing hymns like Amy. Hurting people who hear her play on her harp and sing the truth are soothed and strengthened for the storms of life.

Your church or committee can view clips of me speaking or of Amy singing on our websites. We long to bring this message to as many as possible in an affordable way. Please feel free to contact my manager or Amy's at our web addresses.

We covet your prayers as we carry this message. May the Lord be with you, and help you to comfort others with the comfort you have received. Thanks so much.

Warmly,

DEE BRESTIN, www.deebrestin.com

AMY SHREVE, www.amyshreve.com

The God of All Comfort

Finding Your Way into His Arms

Dee Brestin, Bestselling Author of Falling in Love with Jesus

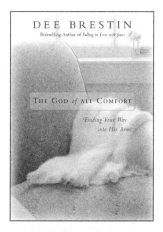

After losing her fifty-nine-year-old husband to cancer, Dee Brestin wondered if her life was over as well. She ached for God's comfort but felt utterly alone.

Then she discovered a secret that suffering souls through the centuries have learned: She began using psalms and classic hymns to speak the truth to her fretful soul. The truths carried by these timeless songs—many of which Brestin includes in this book—can calm the most fretful spirit. They invite the wounded heart to be quiet before God, to rest like a child in the arms of a loving parent.

Each of us must travel down roads of bereavement, betrayal, and broken dreams. *The God of All Comfort* will help readers find their way into the arms of God. With compassion and spiritual wisdom, Brestin draws on the difficult beauty of her own story as well as her skills as a Bible teacher to offer companionship, comfort, and hope.

Hardcover, Jacketed: 978-0-310-29361-3

Pick up a copy at your favorite bookstore or online!

ZONDERVAN®
.com

Share Your Thoughts

With the Author: Your comments will be forwarded to the author when you send them to *zauthor@zondervan.com*.

With Zondervan: Submit your review of this book by writing to *zreview@zondervan.com*.

Free Online Resources at

www.zondervan.com

Zondervan AuthorTracker: Be notified whenever your favorite authors publish new books, go on tour, or post an update about what's happening in their lives at www.zondervan.com/authortracker.

Daily Bible Verses and Devotions: Enrich your life with daily Bible verses or devotions that help you start every morning focused on God. Visit www.zondervan.com/newsletters.

Free Email Publications: Sign up for newsletters on Christian living, academic resources, church ministry, fiction, children's resources, and more. Visit www.zondervan.com/newsletters.

Zondervan Bible Search: Find and compare Bible passages in a variety of translations at www.zondervanbiblesearch.com.

Other Benefits: Register yourself to receive online benefits like coupons and special offers, or to participate in research.

ZONDERVAN®

ZONDERVAN.com/
AUTHOR**TRACKER**
follow your favorite authors